Publishing
P S
Solutions

Oh Sew Cozy Flannel Quilts

Flannel quilt inspirations
for creating inviting, cozy quilts that
are sure to be family favorites.

Lynette Jensen

PS
Publishing
Solutions

Publishing Solutions, LLC

This book was designed, produced and published by Publishing Solutions, LLC.
1107 Hazeltine Boulevard, Suite 470, Chaska, MN 55318

President – James L. Knapp
Creative Director – Lynette Jensen
Art Director – Laurel Albright
Photographer – Craig Anderson
Photostyling – Lynette Jensen
Technical Writer – Sue Bahr
Technical Illustrator – Lisa Kirchoff

We wish to thank the support staff of Thimbleberries® Design Studio: Sherry Husske,
Virginia Brodd, Renae Ashwill, Ardelle Paulson, Kathy Lobeck, Carla Plowman, Julie Jergens,
Pearl Baysinger, Tracy Schrantz, Leone Rusch, Julie Borg, Clarine Howe and Ellen Carter.

Our Promise to You:
All projects in this book have been created in their entirety
by the staff at Thimbleberries Design Studio.
The accuracy of our patterns and instructions have been thoroughly tested.

ISBN: 1-932533-04-4

Printed in the United States of America.

Table of Contents

Table of Contents

Table of Contents

Introduction

Soft, warm, and cozy...
flannel quilts are the best!

Flannel fabrics are fun and easy to use.
The warm, comforting texture of flannel,
combined with rich inviting colors make
flannel a popular choice for cozy quilts.
As a home decor accessory, a flannel quilt
adds warmth and beauty to any room in the
house. These user friendly quilts are the first
choice to ward off an evening chill.

In THIMBLEBERRIES®
Oh Sew Cozy Flannel Quilts,
Lynette Jensen showcases many all-time
favorite quilts. These quilts span the seasons
from Winter Garden to the Picnic Quilt.
The designs are timeless, the texture is
enticing, and the colors are glorious.

Enjoy!

Trip Around The World

Finished Size: 60 x 76"

Fabrics and Supplies

1-1/4 yards **PLUM FLORAL** for quilt center and corner squares

1-5/8 yards **BEIGE FLOWER** for quilt center

1 yard **PLUM PRINT** for quilt center

2/3 yard **GREEN WIDE STRIPE** for inner border

1-1/2 yards **PURPLE WILD ROSE** for outer border

1-5/8 yards **GREEN WIDE STRIPE** for binding

4-1/2 yards backing fabric

quilt batting, at least 64 x 80"

Quilt Center

Cutting

From **PLUM FLORAL**:
- Cut 6, 4-1/2 x 42" strips.
  From 2 of the strips cut:
  12, 4-1/2" squares. The remaining 4 strips will be used for the strip sets.

From **BEIGE FLOWER**:
- Cut 11, 4-1/2 x 42" strips.
  From 3 of the strips cut:
  23, 4-1/2" squares. The remaining 8 strips will be used for the strip sets.

From **PLUM PRINT**:
- Cut 5, 4-1/2 x 42" strips. From the strips cut:
  40, 4-1/2" squares

Piecing

Step 1 Aligning long edges, sew 4-1/2 x 42" **BEIGE FLOWER** strips to both side edges of a 4-1/2 x 42" **PLUM FLORAL** strip. Press the seam allowances toward the dark fabric, referring to Hints and Helps for Pressing Strip Sets on

page 122. Make a total of 4 strip sets. Cut the strip sets into segments.

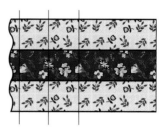

Crosscut 30, 4-1/2" wide segments

Step 2 Referring to the diagram, lay out one of the strip sets, 3 of the 4-1/2" **PLUM FLORAL** squares, 3 of the 4-1/2" **BEIGE FLOWER** squares, and 2 of the 4-1/2" **PLUM PRINT** squares for Section A. Sew the pieces together and press the seam allowances toward the dark fabric.

Strip Set

Section A

Make 4 rows

Step 3 Referring to the diagram, lay out 3 of the strip sets and 2 of the 4-1/2" **PLUM PRINT** squares for Section B. Sew the pieces together and press the seam allowances toward the dark fabric.

Strip Set   *Strip Set*   *Strip Set*

Section B

Make 4 rows

Step 4 Referring to the diagram, lay out 2 of the strip sets, 3 of the 4-1/2" **PLUM PRINT** squares, and 2 of the 4-1/2" **BEIGE FLOWER** squares for Section C. Sew the pieces together and press the seam allowances toward the dark fabric.

Section C

Make 4 rows

Step 5 Referring to the diagram, lay out 2 of the strip sets, 4 of the 4-1/2" **PLUM PRINT** squares, and 1 of the 4-1/2" **BEIGE FLOWER** squares for Section D. Sew the pieces together and press the seam allowances toward the dark fabric.

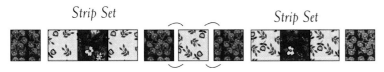

Section D

Make 3 rows

Step 6 Referring to the quilt assembly diagram for placement, lay out the completed sections.

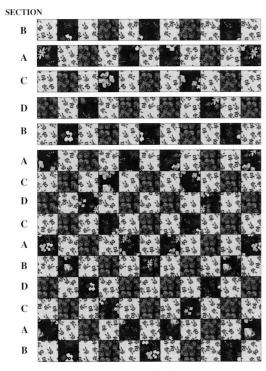

Quilt Assembly Diagram

Step 7 Pin the sections together at the block intersections and stitch. Press the seam

allowances in one direction. <u>At this point the quilt center should measure 44-1/2 x 60-1/2"</u>.

Borders

Note: The yardage given allows for the border strips to be cut on the crosswise grain. Diagonally piece the strips as needed, referring to Diagonal Piecing instructions on page 125. Read through Border instructions on page 125 for general instructions on adding borders.

Cutting

From **GREEN WIDE STRIPE**:
• Cut 6, 2-1/2 x 42" inner border strips

From **PURPLE WILD ROSE**:
• Cut 7, 6-1/2 x 42" outer border strips

From **PLUM FLORAL**:
• Cut 4, 6-1/2" corner squares

Attaching the Borders

Step 1 Attach the 2-1/2" wide **GREEN WIDE STRIPE** inner border strips.

Step 2 To attach the 6-1/2" wide **PURPLE WILD ROSE** outer border strips with 6-1/2" **PLUM FLORAL** corner squares, refer to page 126 for Borders with Corner Squares.

Putting It All Together

Cut the 4-1/2 yard length of backing fabric in half crosswise to make 2, 2-1/4 yard lengths. Refer to Finishing the Quilt on page 126 for complete instructions.

Binding

From **GREEN WIDE STRIPE**:
• Cut 8, 6-1/2 x 42" strips

Sew the binding to the quilt using a scant 1" seam allowance. This measurement will produce a 1" finished double binding. Refer to page 127 for Binding and Diagonal Piecing on page 127 for complete instructions.

Trip Around The World

Winter Garden

Finished Size: 65 x 76"   *Block: 8" square*

Fabrics and Supplies

1 yard	**GREEN PRINT** for pieced blocks
1 yard	**BEIGE PRINT** for pieced blocks
2-3/8 yards	**LARGE BLUE FLORAL** for alternate blocks and outer border
1-3/8 yards	**GOLD FLORAL** for side and corner triangles, and middle border
5/8 yard	**BLUE GRID** for inner border
1-5/8 yards	**GREEN PRINT** for binding
4-1/2 yards	backing fabric

quilt batting, at least 69 x 80"

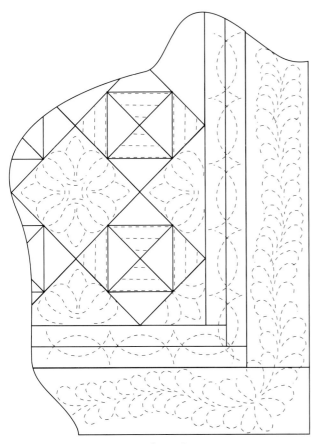

Quilting Suggestion

Pieced Blocks

Make 20 blocks

Cutting

From **GREEN PRINT**:
- Cut 5, 4-7/8 x 42" strips

From **BEIGE PRINT**:
- Cut 5, 4-7/8 x 42" strips

Piecing

Step 1 With right sides together, layer the 4-7/8 x 42" **GREEN PRINT** and **BEIGE PRINT** strips in pairs. Press together, but do not sew. Cut the layered strips into segments.

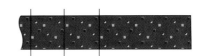

Crosscut 40, 4-7/8-inch squares

Step 2 Cut each layered square in half diagonally to make 80 sets of triangles. Stitch 1/4" from the diagonal edge of each pair of triangles; press. <u>At this point each triangle-pieced square should measure 4-1/2" square.</u>

Make 80, 4-1/2-inch triangle-pieced squares

Step 3 Sew the Step 2 units together in pairs; press. Sew the pairs together to make the pieced block; press. <u>At this point each pieced block should measure 8-1/2" square.</u>

Make 40   *Make 20*

Quilt Center

Note: The side and corner triangles are larger than necessary and will be trimmed before the borders are added.

Cutting

From LARGE BLUE FLORAL:
- Cut 3, 8-1/2 x 42" strips. From the strips cut: 12, 8-1/2" alternate blocks

From GOLD FLORAL:
- Cut 2, 13 x 42" strips. From the strips cut: 4, 13" squares. Cut the squares diagonally into quarters for a total of 16 triangles. You will be using only 14 for side triangles. 2, 8" squares. Cut the squares in half diagonally for a total of 4 corner triangles.

Quilt Center Assembly

Step 1 Referring to quilt diagram, sew together the pieced blocks, alternate blocks, and side triangles in diagonal rows. Press the seam allowances in alternating directions by rows so the seams will fit snugly together with less bulk.

Step 2 Pin the rows at the block intersections and sew the rows together. Press the seam allowances in one direction.

Step 3 Sew the corner triangles to the quilt; press.

Step 4 Trim away the excess fabric from the side and corner triangles, taking care to allow a 1/4" seam allowance beyond the corners of each block. Refer to Trimming Side and Corner Triangles on page 121 for complete instructions.

Borders

Note: The yardage given allows for the border strips to be cut on the crosswise grain. Diagonally piece the strips as needed, referring to Diagonal Piecing instructions on page 125. Read through Border instructions on page 125 for general instructions on adding borders.

Cutting

From BLUE GRID:
- Cut 6, 2-1/2 x 42" inner border strips

From GOLD FLORAL:
- Cut 6, 2-1/2 x 42" middle border strips

From LARGE BLUE FLORAL:
- Cut 8, 6-1/2 x 42" outer border strips

Attaching the Borders

Step 1 Attach the 2-1/2" wide **BLUE GRID** inner border strips.

Step 2 Attach the 2-1/2" wide **GOLD FLORAL** middle border strips.

Step 3 Attach the 6-1/2" wide **LARGE BLUE FLORAL** outer border strips.

Putting It All Together

Cut the 4-1/2 yard length of backing fabric in half crosswise to make 2, 2-1/4 yard lengths. Refer to Finishing the Quilt on page 126 for complete instructions.

Binding

Cutting

From GREEN PRINT:
- Cut 8, 6-1/2 x 42-inch strips

Sew the binding to the quilt using a scant 1" seam allowance. This measurement will produce a 1" wide finished double binding. Refer to Binding and Diagonal Piecing instructions on page 127 for complete instructions.

Winter Garden

Sleepy Time

Finished Size: 74 x 92"   Block: 8 x 14"

Fabrics and Supplies

5/8 yard   **RED PRINT** for blocks

5/8 yard   **GREEN PRINT** for blocks

7/8 yard   **BEIGE PRINT** for blocks

4 yards   **BEIGE MITTEN PRINT**
for alternate blocks and border
(cut on lengthwise grain)

1-1/2 yards   **GREEN FLORAL** for lattice strips

1/3 yard   **GOLD PRINT** for lattice posts

1-7/8 yards   **RED PLAID** for binding
(cut on the bias)

5-1/2 yards   backing fabric

quilt batting, at least 78 x 96"

Block A

Make 8 blocks

Cutting

From **RED PRINT**:
- Cut 2, 4-1/2 x 42" strips

From **GREEN PRINT**:
- Cut 2, 4-1/2 x 42" strips

From **BEIGE PRINT**:
- Cut 2, 6-1/2 x 42" strips. From the strips cut:
  8, 6-1/2 x 8-1/2" rectangles

Piecing

Step 1 Aligning long edges, sew the 4-1/2 x 42"
RED PRINT and **GREEN PRINT**
strips together in pairs. Press, referring
to page 122 for Hints and Helps for
Pressing Strip Sets. Make a total of 2 strip
sets. Cut the strip sets into segments.

Crosscut 16, 4-1/2" wide segments

Step 2 Sew the Step 1 segments together in pairs;
press. <u>At this point each four-patch unit
should measure 8-1/2" square.</u>

Make 8 four-patch units

Step 3 Sew a 6-1/2 x 8-1/2" **BEIGE PRINT**
rectangle to the top of each four-patch
unit; press. <u>At this point each Block A
should measure 8-1/2 x 14-1/2".</u>

Block A   Make 8

Block B

Make 8 blocks

Cutting

From **RED PRINT**:
 • Cut 2, 4-1/2 x 42" strips

From **GREEN PRINT**:
 • Cut 2, 4-1/2 x 42" strips

From **BEIGE PRINT**:
 • Cut 2, 6-1/2 x 42" strips. From the strips cut:
 8, 6-1/2 x 8-1/2" rectangles

Piecing

Step 1 Aligning long edges, sew the 4-1/2 x 42"
RED PRINT and **GREEN PRINT** strips
together in pairs; press. Make a total of 2
strip sets. Cut the strip sets into segments.

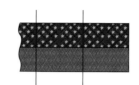

Crosscut 8, 8-1/2" wide segments

Step 2 Sew a 6-1/2 x 8-1/2" **BEIGE PRINT** rectangle to the bottom of each Step 1 segment;
press. <u>At this point each Block B should
measure 8-1/2 x 14-1/2".</u>

Block B   Make 8

Quilt Center

*Note: The yardage given allows for the BEIGE MITTEN
PRINT border strips to be cut on the lengthwise grain (a
couple extra inches are allowed for trimming). Set them
aside to be attached to the quilt center later. Cutting the
strips on the lengthwise grain will eliminate the need for
piecing. The yardage given allows for the lattice strips to be
cut on the crosswise grain. Read through Border instructions
on page 125 for general instructions on adding borders.*

Cutting

From **BEIGE MITTEN PRINT**:
 • Cut 2, 8-1/2 x 100" side outer border
 strips (cut on lengthwise grain)

 • Cut 2, 8-1/2 x 62" top/bottom outer
 border strips (cut on lengthwise grain).
 Set the 4 outer border strips aside.

 • Cut 6, 6-1/2 x 42" strips
 (cut on crosswise grain).
 From the strips cut:
 12, 6-1/2 x 14-1/2" alternate block rectangles

From **GREEN FLORAL**:
- Cut 7, 4-1/2 x 42" strips.
  From the strips cut:
  5, 4-1/2 x 50-1/2" lattice strips

- Cut 4, 4-1/2 x 42" strips.
  From the strips cut:
  8, 4-1/2 x 14-1/2" lattice strips

From **GOLD PRINT**:
- Cut 2, 4-1/2 x 42" strips.
  From the strips cut:
  10, 4-1/2" lattice posts

Quilt Center Assembly

Step 1 Referring to the diagram for block placement, sew 2 of the A Blocks, 2 of the B Blocks, and 3 of the 6-1/2 x 14-1/2" **BEIGE MITTEN PRINT** rectangles together in a row. Sew a 4-1/2 x 14-1/2" **GREEN FLORAL** lattice strip to both ends of the block row; press. Make 2 block rows. At this point each block row should measure 14-1/2 x 58-1/2".

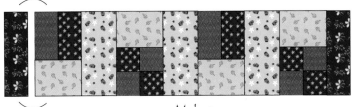

Make 2

Step 2 Referring to the diagram for block placement, sew 2 of the A Blocks, 2 of the B Blocks, and 3 of the 6-1/2 x 14-1/2" **BEIGE MITTEN PRINT** rectangles together in a row. Sew a 4-1/2 x 14-1/2" **GREEN FLORAL** lattice strip to both ends of the block row, press. Make 2 block rows. At this point each block row should measure 14-1/2 x 58-1/2".

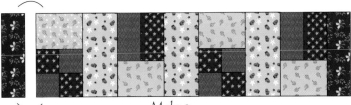

Make 2

Step 3 Sew a 4-1/2" **GOLD PRINT** lattice post square to both ends of each 4-1/2 x 50-1/2" **GREEN FLORAL** lattice strip; press. Make a total of 5 lattice strips. At this point each lattice strip should measure 4-1/2 x 58-1/2".

Step 4 Referring to the quilt diagram, sew the block rows and lattice strips together; press.

Border

Note: The BEIGE MITTEN PRINT outer border strips were cut in the Quilt Center section.

Attaching the Border

To attach the 8-1/2" wide **BEIGE MITTEN PRINT** border strips, refer to page 125 for Border instructions.

Putting It All Together

Cut the 5-1/2 yard length of backing fabric in half crosswise to make 2, 2-3/4 yard lengths. Refer to Finishing the Quilt on page 126 for complete instructions.

Binding

Cutting

From RED PLAID:
- Cut enough 6-1/2" wide bias strips to make a 350" long strip

Sew the binding to the quilt using a scant 1" seam allowance. This measurement will produce a 1" wide finished double binding. Refer to Binding and Diagonal Piecing instructions on page 127 for complete instructions.

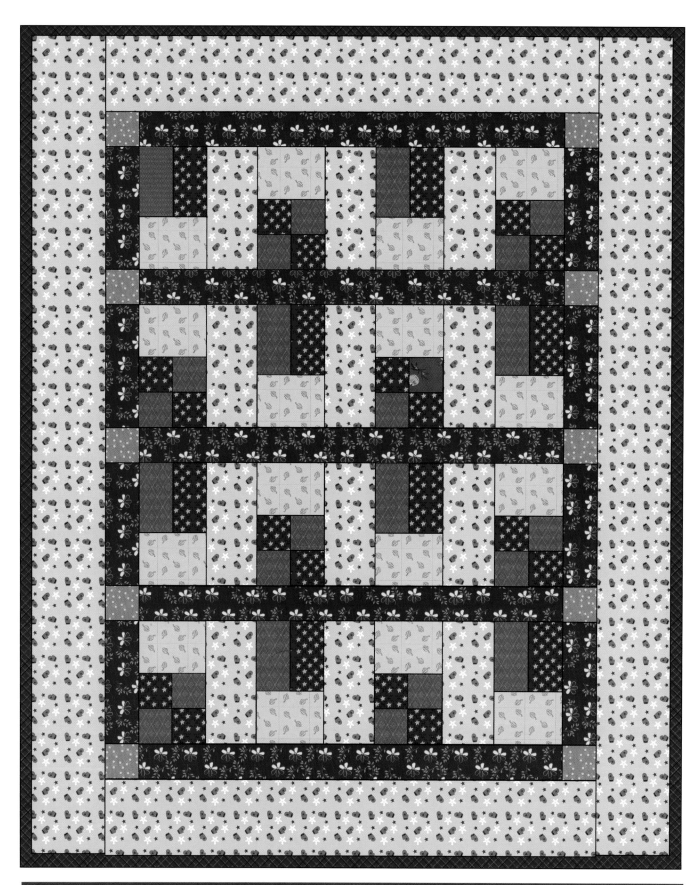

Sleepy Time

Fabrics and Supplies

1-3/8 yards GREEN PRINT
for pillow front and back

1/3 yard BEIGE PRINT for pillow flap

5, 1" diameter buttons

20" square pillow form

Cutting

From GREEN PRINT:
- Cut 2, 21 x 26" rectangles for pillow back
- Cut 1, 21" square for pillow front

From BEIGE PRINT:
- Cut 1, 10 x 21" rectangle for mock flap

Assembly

Step 1 With wrong sides together, fold the 10 x 21" BEIGE PRINT rectangle in half lengthwise; and press.

Step 2 With raw edges aligned, position the folded rectangle on the right side of the 21" GREEN PRINT square; baste the flap in place.

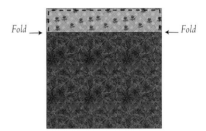

Step 3 With wrong sides together, fold each 21 x 26" GREEN PRINT rectangle in half to make 2, 13 x 21" double-thick pillow back pieces. Overlap the 2 folded edges so the pillow back measures 21" square; pin. Stitch around the entire piece to create a single pillow back, using a 1/4" seam allowance.

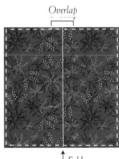

Step 4 With right sides together, layer the pillow back and the pillow front, and pin. Stitch around the outside edges using a 1/2" seam allowance.

Step 5 Trim the pillow back and corner seam allowances if needed. Turn the pillow right side out. Position the 5 buttons on the flap; stitch in place. Insert the pillow form through the back opening.

Toastie Toes

Finished Size: 56 x 72"   Block: 8" square

5/8 yard **GREEN MITTEN PRINT** for Block A

7/8 yard **RED PRINT** for Block A

5/8 yard **MEDIUM GOLD PRINT** for Block A

1/2 yard **BLACK FLORAL** for Block B

1/2 yard **RED APPLE PRINT** for Block B

3/4 yard **DARK GOLD PRINT** for Block B

1 yard **BEIGE MITTEN PRINT** for inner border

1-1/8 yards **GREEN PRINT** for outer border

1-3/8 yards **BLACK FLORAL** for binding

3-1/2 yards backing fabric

quilt batting, at least 60 x 76"

pearl cotton or machine embroidery thread for decorative stitches; black

Block A

Make 18 blocks

Cutting

From **GREEN MITTEN PRINT**:
• Cut 3, 4-1/2 x 42" strips

From **RED PRINT**:
• Cut 9, 2-1/2 x 42" strips. From the strips cut: 36, 2-1/2 x 8-1/2" rectangles

From **MEDIUM GOLD PRINT**:
• Cut 3, 4-1/2 x 42" strips

Piecing

Step 1 Aligning long edges, sew the 4-1/2 x 42" **GREEN MITTEN PRINT** strips and **MEDIUM GOLD PRINT** strips together in pairs. Press the seam allowances open for ease in adding a decorative stitch along the seam line. Make 3 strip sets. *See note below to add decorative stitching. After decorative stitching is added, cut the strip sets into segments.

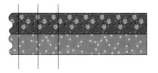

Crosscut 18, 4-1/2" wide segments

Note: At this point, a decorative stitch can be added along the seam line. We added a machine feather stitch using Mettler® embroidery thread for the top thread and regular sewing thread in the bobbin. If you like, you could stitch this by hand. Refer to the Decorative Stitch Diagram.

Step 2 Sew a 2-1/2 x 8-1/2" **RED PRINT** rectangle to both side edges of the Step 1 segments; press open. As in Step 1, a decorative stitch may be added along the seam line at this time. <u>At this point each block should measure 8-1/2" square.</u>

 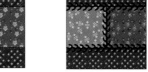

Block A   *Make 18 with feather stitch*

Block B

Make 17 blocks

Cutting

From **BLACK FLORAL**:
- Cut 5, 2-1/2 x 42" strips

From **RED APPLE PRINT**:
- Cut 5, 2-1/2 x 42" strips

From **DARK GOLD PRINT**:
- Cut 5, 4-1/2 x 42" strips

Piecing

Step 1 Aligning long edges, sew a 2-1/2 x 42" **BLACK FLORAL** strip to the top edge of a 4-1/2 x 42" **DARK GOLD PRINT** strip. Sew a 2-1/2 x 42" **RED APPLE PRINT** strip to the bottom edge of this strip. Press the seam allowances open. Make 5 strip sets. At this point a decorative stitch can be added along the seam lines. Cut the strip sets into segments. <u>At this point each Block B should measure 8-1/2" square.</u>

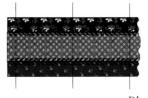

Feather stitch strips and

Crosscut 17, 8-1/2" wide segments

Block B

Quilt Center Assembly

Step 1 The quilt is assembled in 7 horizontal rows of 5 blocks each. Referring to the diagrams, sew Blocks A and Blocks B together in rows; press. Press the seam allowances toward the B Blocks.

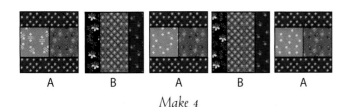

Make 4

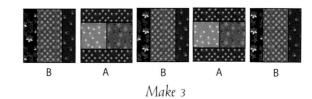

Make 3

Step 2 Referring to the quilt diagram, lay out the block rows. Pin the rows together at the block intersections. Sew the rows together; press.

Borders

Note: The yardage given allows for the border strips to be cut on the crosswise grain. Diagonally piece the strips together as needed, referring to Diagonal Piecing instructions on page 125.

Cutting

From **BEIGE MITTEN PRINT**:
- Cut 6, 4-1/2 x 42" inner border strips

From **GREEN PRINT**:
- Cut 7, 4-1/2 x 42" outer border strips

Attaching the Borders

Step 1 Attach the 4-1/2" wide **BEIGE MITTEN PRINT** inner border strips.

Step 2 Attach the 4-1/2" wide **GREEN PRINT** outer border strips.

Putting It All Together

Cut the 3-1/2 yard length of backing fabric in half crosswise to make 2, 1-3/4 yard lengths. Refer to Finishing the Quilt on page 126 for complete instructions.

Binding

Cutting

From **BLACK FLORAL**:
- Cut 7, 6-1/2 x 42" strips

Sew the binding to the quilt using a scant 1" seam allowance. This measurement will produce a 1" wide finished double binding. Refer to Binding and Diagonal Piecing on page 127 for complete instructions.

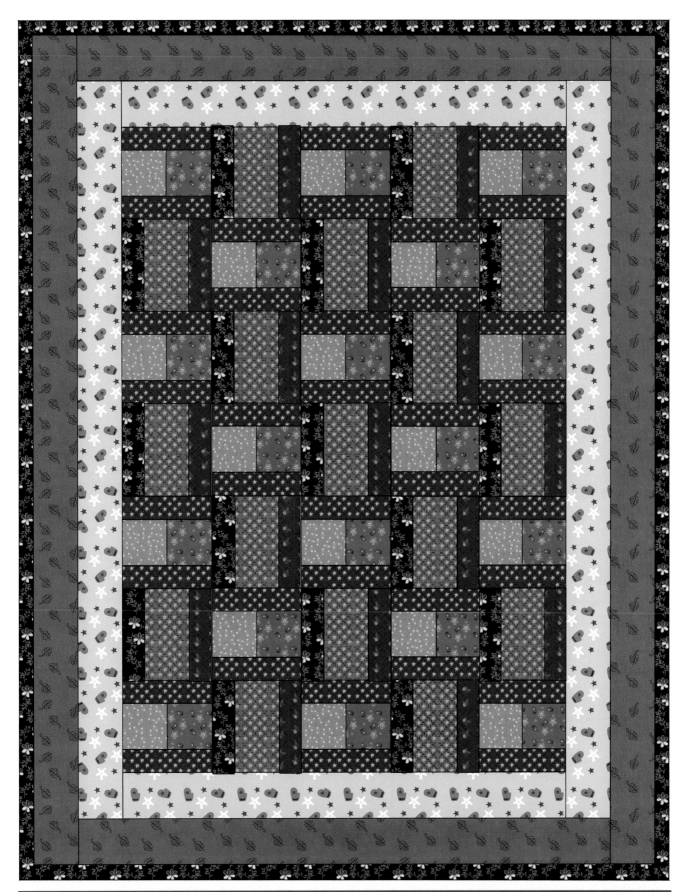

Toastie Toes

Timberline

Finished Size: 76 x 92"

Fabrics and Supplies

2-5/8 yards **BLUE PRINT** for hourglass blocks, house bases, and outer border

3/8 yard **BEIGE CHECK** for hourglass blocks

2-1/2 yards **BEIGE LILY PRINT** for hourglass blocks and background

3/8 yard **BEIGE PLAID** for hourglass blocks

1-1/2 yards **RED PRINT** for inner borders and corner squares

1/2 yard **RED PLAID** for roofs

1/3 yard **GOLD STRIPE** for windows

2 yards **GREEN PRINT** for trees, middle border, and corner squares

1/8 yard **DARK GREEN STRIPE** for trunks

2 yards **RED PLAID** for binding (cut on the bias)

5-1/3 yards backing fabric

quilt batting, at least 80 x 96"

Hourglass Blocks and Inner Border

Make 7 **BLUE/BEIGE CHECK** blocks

Make 8 **BEIGE PLAID/BEIGE LILY PRINT** blocks

Cutting

From **BLUE PRINT**:
- Cut 1, 9-1/4 x 42" strip. From the strip cut: 4, 9-1/4" squares. Cut the squares diagonally into quarters for a total of 16 triangles. You will be using only 14 triangles.

From **BEIGE CHECK**:
- Cut 1, 9-1/4 x 42" strip. From the strip cut: 4, 9-1/4" squares. Cut the squares diagonally into quarters for a total of 16 triangles. You will be using only 14 triangles.

From **BEIGE PLAID**:
- Cut 1, 9-1/4 x 42" strip. From the strip cut: 4, 9-1/4" squares. Cut the squares diagonally into quarters for a total of 16 triangles.

From **BEIGE LILY PRINT**:
- Cut 1, 9-1/4 x 42" strip. From the strip cut: 4, 9-1/4" squares. Cut the squares diagonally into quarters for a total of 16 triangles.

From **RED PRINT**:
- Cut 5, 4-1/2 x 42" inner border strips

Quilt Center Assembly

Step 1 Layer a **BLUE PRINT** triangle on a **BEIGE CHECK** triangle. Stitch along the bias edge; press. Repeat with the remaining **BLUE PRINT** and **BEIGE CHECK** triangles, stitching along the same bias edge of each triangle set. Sew the triangle units together in pairs; press. <u>At this point each hourglass block should measure 8-1/2" square.</u>

Bias edges

Make 14   *Make 7*

Step 2 Layer a **BEIGE PLAID** triangle on a **BEIGE LILY PRINT** triangle. Stitch along the bias edge; press. Repeat with the remaining **BEIGE PLAID** and **BEIGE LILY PRINT** triangles, stitching along the same bias edge of each triangle set. Sew the triangle units together in pairs; press. <u>At this point each hourglass block should measure 8-1/2" square.</u>

Bias edges

Make 16   *Make 8*

Step 3 Referring to the quilt diagram, sew the Step 1 and Step 2 hourglass blocks together in rows. Press the seam allowances in alternating directions by rows so the seams will fit snugly together with less bulk. Pin the rows at the block intersections and sew the rows together. Press the seam allowances in one direction. <u>At this point the quilt center should measure 24-1/2 x 40-1/2".</u>

Step 4 Attach the 4-1/2" wide **RED PRINT** inner border strips.

Assemble and Attach the Roof Sections

Cutting

From RED PLAID:
- Cut 3, 4-1/2 x 42" strips. From the strips cut: 10, 4-1/2 x 8-1/2" rectangles

From BEIGE LILY PRINT:
- Cut 6, 4-1/2 x 42" strips. From the strips cut: 10, 4-1/2 x 8-1/2" rectangles 24, 4-1/2" squares

Assembling and Attaching the Borders

Step 1 Position a 4-1/2" **BEIGE LILY PRINT** square on the corner of a 4-1/2 x 8-1/2" **RED PLAID** rectangle. Draw a diagonal line on the square and stitch on the line. Trim the seam allowance to 1/4"; press. Repeat this process at the opposite corner of the rectangle. <u>At this point each roof unit should measure 4-1/2 x 8-1/2".</u>

Make 10

Step 2 To make the top/bottom roof sections, sew together 2 of the roof units, one of the 4-1/2 x 8-1/2" **BEIGE LILY PRINT** rectangles, and 2 of the 4-1/2" **BEIGE LILY PRINT** squares; press. <u>At this point each roof section should measure 4-1/2 x 32-1/2".</u> Sew these sections to the quilt center; press.

Make 2

Step 3 To make the side roof sections, sew together 3 of the roof units and 4 of the 4-1/2 x 8-1/2" **BEIGE LILY PRINT** rectangles; press. <u>At this point each roof section should measure 4-1/2 x 56-1/2".</u> Sew these sections to the quilt center; press.

Make 2

House Base

Make 10 house bases

Cutting

From BLUE PRINT:
- Cut 2, 4-1/2 x 42" strips
- Cut 2, 2-1/2 x 42" strips
- Cut 7 more 2-1/2 x 42" strips. From the strips cut: 20, 2-1/2 x 10-1/2" rectangles

From GOLD STRIPE:
- Cut 2, 4-1/2 x 42" strips

Piecing

Step 1 Aligning long edges, sew a 2-1/2 x 42" **BLUE PRINT** strip to a 4-1/2 x 42" **GOLD STRIPE** strip. Sew a 4-1/2 x 42" **BLUE PRINT** strip to the opposite side of the **GOLD STRIPE** strip. Press the seam allowances toward the **BLUE PRINT** strips. Make a total of 2 strip sets. Cut the strip sets into segments.

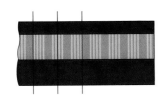

Crosscut 10, 4-1/2" wide segments

Step 2 Sew 2-1/2 x 10-1/2" **BLUE PRINT** rectangles to both side edges of the Step 1 units; press. <u>At this point each house base should measure 8-1/2 x 10-1/2"</u>.

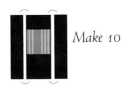   *Make 10*

Tree Blocks

Make 14 blocks

Cutting

From **GREEN PRINT**:

- Cut 4, 4-1/2 x 42" strips.
  From the strips cut:
  14, 4-1/2 x 8-1/2" rectangles

- Cut 7, 2-1/2 x 42" strips.From the strips cut:
  28, 2-1/2 x 8-1/2" rectangles

From **BEIGE LILY PRINT**:

- Cut 4, 4-1/2 x 42" strips. From the strips cut:
  28, 4-1/2" squares

- Cut 2, 3-1/2 x 42" strips

- Cut 4, 2-1/2 x 42" strips. From the strips cut:
  56, 2-1/2" squares

From **DARK GREEN STRIPE**:

- Cut 1, 2-1/2 x 42" strip

Piecing

Step 1 Position a 4-1/2" **BEIGE LILY PRINT** square on the corner of a 4-1/2 x 8-1/2" **GREEN PRINT** rectangle. Draw a diagonal line on the square, stitch, trim, and press. Repeat this process at the opposite corner of the rectangle. <u>At this point each unit should measure 4-1/2 x 8-1/2"</u>.

Make 14

Step 2 Position 2-1/2" **BEIGE LILY PRINT** squares on both corners of a 2-1/2 x 8-1/2" **GREEN PRINT** rectangle. Draw a diagonal line on the **BEIGE LILY PRINT** squares, stitch, trim, and press. <u>At this point each unit should measure 2-1/2 x 8-1/2"</u>.

Make 28

Step 3 Aligning long edges, sew 2 of the 3-1/2 x 42" **BEIGE LILY PRINT** strips to both side edges of the 2-1/2 x 42" **DARK GREEN STRIPE** strip. Press the seam allowances toward the **DARK GREEN STRIPE** strip.

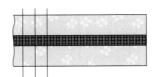

Crosscut 14, 2-1/2" wide segments

Step 4 Referring to the block diagram, sew together the Step 1, 2, and 3 units; press. <u>At this point each tree block should measure 8-1/2 x 10-1/2".</u>

Make 14

Quilt Center

Cutting

From **RED PRINT**:
- Cut 1, 4-1/2 x 42" strip. From the strip cut: 4, 4-1/2" squares

From **GREEN PRINT**:
- Cut 1, 6-1/2 x 42" strip. From the strip cut: 4, 6-1/2" squares

From **BEIGE LILY PRINT**:
- Cut 2, 4-1/2 x 42" strips. From the strips cut: 8, 4-1/2 x 6-1/2" rectangles

Piecing

Step 1 To make the top/bottom house/tree units, sew together 2 of the house bases and 3 of the tree blocks; press. Make 2 units. <u>At this point each unit should measure 10-1/2 x 40-1/2".</u> Sew these units to the quilt center; press.

Step 2 To make the side house/tree units, sew together 3 of the house bases and 4 of the tree blocks; press. Make 2 units. <u>At this point each unit should measure 10-1/2 x 56-1/2".</u>

Step 3 To make the corner blocks, sew together a 4-1/2 x 6-1/2" **BEIGE LILY PRINT** rectangle and a 4-1/2" **RED PRINT** square; press. Then sew together a 6-1/2" **GREEN PRINT** square and a 4-1/2 x 6-1/2" **BEIGE LILY PRINT** rectangle; press. Sew the 2 units together; press. <u>At this point each corner block should measure 10-1/2" square.</u>

 ( )

Make 4

Step 4 Sew a corner block to both ends of the Step 2 house/tree units; press. Sew these units to the quilt center; press.

Borders

Note: The yardage given allows for the border strips to be cut on the crosswise grain. Diagonally piece the strips as needed, referring to Diagonal Piecing instructions on page 125. Read through Border instructions on page 125 for general instructions on adding borders.

Cutting

From **RED PRINT**:
- Cut 8, 2-1/2 x 42" inner border strips

From **GREEN PRINT**:
- Cut 9, 2-1/2 x 42" middle border strips

From **BLUE PRINT**:
- Cut 10, 4-1/2 x 42" outer border strips

Attaching the Borders

Step 1 Attach the 2-1/2" wide **RED PRINT** inner border strips.

Step 2 Attach the 2-1/2" wide **GREEN PRINT** middle border strips.

Step 3 Attach the 4-1/2" wide **BLUE PRINT** outer border strips.

Putting It All Together

Cut the 5-1/3 yard length of backing fabric in half crosswise to make 2, 2-2/3 yard lengths. Refer to Finishing the Quilt on page 126 for complete instructions.

Binding

Cutting

From **RED PLAID**:
- Cut enough 6-1/2" wide bias strips to make a 350" long strip

Sew the binding to the quilt using a scant 1" seam allowance. This measurement will produce a 1" wide finished double binding. Refer to Binding and Diagonal Piecing on page 127 for complete instructions.

Timberline

Ruffled Pillow Sham

20 x 29" without ruffle

Fabrics and Supplies

3/4yard   for pillow front

1-1/8yards   for pillow ruffle

1-1/8yards   for pillow back

Quilting thread for gathering ruffle

Queen bed pillow form (20 x 29")

Cutting

From **GREEN PRINT**:

• Cut 1, 21 x 30" pillow top rectangle

• Cut 2, 21 x 36" pillow back rectangles

• Cut 6, 6-1/2 x 42" ruffle strips

Attach the Ruffle

Step 1 Diagonally piece together the 6-1/2" wide **GREEN PRINT** ruffle strips to make a continuous ruffle strip, referring to Diagonal Piecing on page 127.

Step 2 Fold the strip in half lengthwise, wrong sides together; press. Divide the ruffle strip into 4 equal segments, and mark the quarter points with safety pins.

Step 3 To gather the ruffle, position quilting thread (or pearl cotton) 1/4" from the raw edges of the folded ruffle strip. You will need a length of thread 200" long. Secure one end of the thread by stitching across it. Zigzag stitch over the thread all the way around the ruffle strip, taking care not to sew through it.

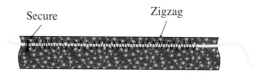

Secure   Zigzag

Step 4 Divide the edges of the 21 x 30" pillow front rectangle into 4 equal segments and mark the quarter points with safety pins. With right sides together and raw edges aligned, pin the ruffle to the pillow top, matching the quarter points. Pull up the gathering stitches until the ruffle fits the pillow front, taking care to allow extra fullness in the ruffle at each corner. Sew the ruffle to the pillow front, using a 1/4" seam allowance.

Assembling the Pillow Back

Step 1 With wrong sides together, fold each 21 x 36" pillow back rectangle in half crosswise to form 2, 18 x 21" double-thick pillow back pieces. Overlap the 2 folded edges so the pillow back measures 21 x 30". Pin the pieces together and stitch around the entire piece to create a single pillow back, using a scant 1/4" seam allowance.

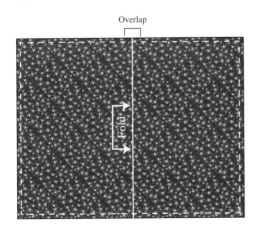

Step 2 With right sides together, layer the pillow back and the pillow front; pin. The ruffle

will be sandwiched between the 2 layers and turned toward the center of the pillow at this time. Pin and stitch around the outside edges using a 1/2" seam allowance.

Step 3 Turn the pillow sham right side out, insert the pillow form through the pillow back opening, and fluff up the ruffle.

Cuddle Up

Finished Size: 72 x 86"   Block: 6 x 8"

Fabrics and Supplies

1 yard   **BEIGE FLORAL** for Block A

1 yard   **BLUE PRINT** for Blocks A and B,
            and corner squares

1 yard   **BROWN LEAF** print for
            Blocks A and B

1 yard   **BLUE FLORAL** for Blocks A and B

2 yards   **GOLD STRIPE** for lattice pieces
            and strips

2-2/3 yards **BLUE PLAID** for outer border
            (cut on the lengthwise grain)

1-3/4 yards **BLUE PRINT** for binding

5-1/4 yards backing fabric

quilt batting, at least 76 x 90"

Block A

Make 25 blocks

Cutting

From **BEIGE FLORAL**:
- Cut 9, 2-1/2 x 42" strips

From **BLUE PRINT**:
- Cut 3, 2-1/2 x 42" strips

From **BROWN LEAF PRINT**:
- Cut 3, 2-1/2 x 42" strips

From **BLUE FLORAL**:
- Cut 3, 2-1/2 x 42" strips

Piecing

Step 1 Aligning long edges, sew a 2-1/2" wide **BEIGE FLORAL** strip to both side edges of a 2-1/2" wide **BLUE PRINT** strip. Press the seam allowances toward the **BLUE PRINT** strip, referring to Hints and Helps for Pressing Strip Sets on page 122. Make 3 strip sets. Cut the strip sets into segments.

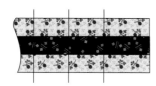

Crosscut 25, 4-1/2" wide segments

Step 2 Aligning long edges, sew a 2-1/2" wide **BLUE FLORAL** strip and a 2-1/2" wide **BROWN LEAF PRINT** strip to both side edges of a 2-1/2" wide **BEIGE FLORAL** strip. Press the seam allowances away from the **BEIGE FLORAL** strip. Make 3 strip sets. Cut the strip sets into segments.

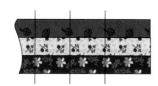

Crosscut 25, 4-1/2" wide segments

Step 3 Sew the Step 1 and Step 2 segments together to make Block A. <u>At this point each Block A should measure 6-1/2 x 8-1/2".</u>

Block A   Make 25

Block B

Make 24 blocks

Cutting

From **BLUE PRINT**:
- Cut 6, 2-1/2 x 42" strips

From **BROWN LEAF PRINT**:
- Cut 6, 2-1/2 x 42" strips

From **BLUE FLORAL**:
- Cut 6, 2-1/2 x 42" strips

Piecing

Aligning long edges, sew a 2-1/2" wide **BLUE FLORAL** strip and a 2-1/2" wide **BROWN LEAF PRINT** strip to both side edges of a 2-1/2" wide **BLUE PRINT** strip. Press the seam allowances toward the **BLUE PRINT** strip. Make 6 strip sets. Cut the strip sets into segments. <u>At this point each Block B should measure 6-1/2 x 8-1/2".</u>

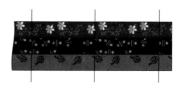

Crosscut 24, 8-1/2" wide segments

Block B   Make 24

Quilt Center and Inner Border

Cutting

From **GOLD STRIPE**:

- Cut 10, 2-1/2 x 42" strips. From the strips cut: 56, 2-1/2 x 6-1/2" lattice pieces
- Cut 16, 2-1/2 x 42" lattice/inner border strips

Quilt Center Assembly

Step 1 To assemble each vertical row, refer to quilt diagram for block placement. Sew together 7 of the pieced blocks and 8 of the lattice pieces. Press the seam allowances toward the lattice pieces. Make 7 block rows. At this point each vertical block row should measure 6-1/2 x 72-1/2".

Note: The block rows must all be the same length. Adjust the seam allowances if needed.

Step 2 Diagonally piece the remaining 2-1/2" wide **GOLD STRIPE** strips. Cut 8, 2-1/2 x 72-1/2" lattice/side inner border strips (or the length of your block rows). Sew together the strips and the block rows; press.

Outer Border

Note: The yardage given allows for the BLUE PLAID outer border strips to be cut on the lengthwise grain (a couple extra inches are allowed for trimming). Cutting the strips on the lengthwise grain will eliminate the need for piecing and matching the plaid. The yardage given allows for the BLUE PRINT strip to be cut on the crosswise grain. Read through Border instructions on page 125 for general instructions on adding borders.

Cutting

From **BLUE PLAID**:

- Cut 2, 7-1/2 x 90" side outer border strips
- Cut 2, 7-1/2 x 61" top/bottom outer border strips

From **BLUE PRINT**:

- Cut 1, 7-1/2 x 42" strip. From the strip cut: 4, 7-1/2" corner squares

Attaching the Outer Border

Step 1 Attach the 7-1/2" wide top/bottom **BLUE PLAID** outer border strips.

Step 2 Attach the 7-1/2" wide side **BLUE PLAID** outer border strips with 7-1/2" **BLUE PRINT** corner squares, referring to Borders with Corner Squares on page 126.

Putting It All Together

Cut the 5-1/4 yard length of backing fabric in half crosswise to make 2, 2-5/8 yard lengths. Refer to Finishing the Quilt on page 126 for complete instructions.

Binding

Cutting

From **BLUE PRINT**:

- Cut 9, 6-1/2 x 42" strips

Sew the binding to the quilt using a scant 1" seam allowance. This measurement will produce a 1" wide finished double binding. Refer to Binding and Diagonal Piecing on page 127 for complete instructions .

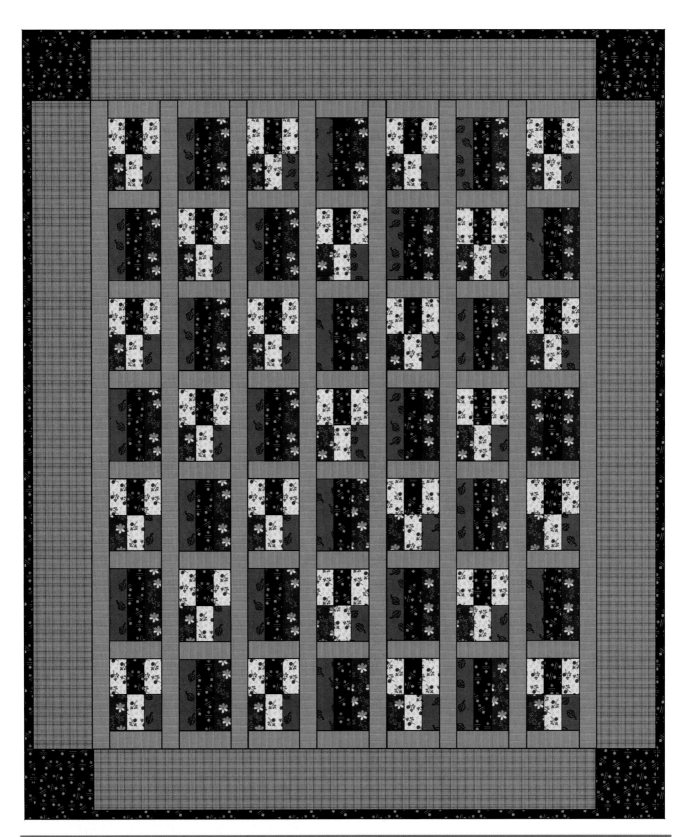

Cuddle Up

Fabrics and Supplies
for one pillow sham

1-7/8 yards **BLUE PRINT** for pillow top
and pillow back

1-1/8 yards **GOLD STRIPE** for pillow ruffle

2/3 yard **MUSLIN** lining for quilted
pillow top

Quilting thread or pearl cotton for gathering ruffle

Gold top-stitching thread

Quilt batting, at least 23 x 32"

Queen bed pillow form (20 x 29")

Cutting

From **BLUE PRINT**:
• Cut 1, 23 x 32" pillow top rectangle
• Cut 2, 21 x 36" pillow back rectangles

From **GOLD STRIPE**:
• Cut 6, 6-1/2 x 42" ruffle strips

From **MUSLIN** lining and quilt batting:
• Cut 1, 23 x 32" rectangle

Quilt the Pillow Top

Step 1 Mark the pillow top with diagonal lines, 2" apart and at a 45° angle creating a crosshatch design (see photo).

Step 2 To prepare the fabric for quilting, layer the 23 x 32" **BLUE PRINT** rectangle, and the 23 x 32" batting and muslin lining rectangles with right sides facing out. Hand-baste (or spray baste) the layers together.

Step 3 Using a walking foot, a 1/4" width double needle, and top-stitching thread, stitch the diagonal markings creating the crosshatch design.

Step 4 When quilting is complete, trim the excess lining and batting to a 21 x 30" rectangle. To prepare the pillow top before attaching the ruffle, I suggest hand-basting the edges of all 3 layers of the quilted pillow top together. This will prevent the edge of the pillow top from rippling when you attach the ruffle.

Attach the Ruffle

Refer to Prairie Point Pillow Sham on page 54 for complete instructions and diagram.

Assembling the Pillow Back

Refer to Prairie Point Pillow Sham on page 54 for complete instructions and diagram.

Flannel Reflections

Finished Size: 90 x 102"   Block: 6" square

Fabrics and Supplies

4-1/8 yards **RED WILD ROSE** for alternate blocks, corner squares, and outer border

2-2/3 yards **BEIGE FLORAL** for triangle-pieced square blocks and middle border

1-3/8 yards **LIGHT GREEN PRINT** for triangle-pieced square blocks

1-3/8 yards **DARK GREEN PRINT** for inner and middle borders

7/8 yard **GOLD STRIPE** for middle border

2-1/4 yards **DARK GREEN PRINT** for binding

8 yards backing fabric

quilt batting, at least 94 x 106"

Quilt Center

Make 49 triangle-pieced square blocks

Cutting

From **RED WILD ROSE**:
- Cut 9, 6-1/2 x 42" strips. From the strips cut: 50, 6-1/2" alternate block squares

From **BEIGE FLORAL**:
- Cut 5, 6-7/8 x 42" strips

From **LIGHT GREEN PRINT**:
- Cut 5, 6-7/8 x 42" strips

Quilt Center Assembly

Step 1 With right sides together, layer the 6-7/8 x 42" **BEIGE FLORAL** and **LIGHT GREEN PRINT** strips together in pairs. Press together, but do not sew. Cut the layered strips into squares. Cut the layered squares in half diagonally to make 49 sets of triangles (there will be one extra set). Stitch 1/4" from the diagonal edge of each pair of triangles; press. <u>At this point each triangle-pieced square block should measure 6-1/2" square.</u>

Crosscut 25, 6-7/8" squares

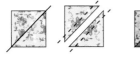

Make 49, 6-1/2" triangle-pieced square blocks

Step 2 Referring to the quilt assembly diagram for block placement, lay out the 6-1/2" **RED WILD ROSE** alternate blocks and the triangle-pieced square blocks in 11 horizontal rows. Sew the blocks together in each row and press the seam allowances toward the alternate blocks.

Step 3 Pin the rows together at the block intersections. Sew the rows together and press the seam allowances in one direction. <u>At this point the quilt center should measure 54-1/2 x 66-1/2".</u>

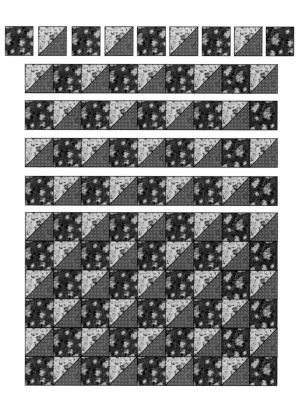

Borders

Note: The yardage given allows for the border strips to be cut on the crosswise grain. Diagonally piece the strips as needed, referring to Diagonal Piecing instructions on page 125. Read through Border instructions on page 125 for general instructions on adding borders.

Cutting

From **DARK GREEN PRINT**:
- Cut 15, 2-1/2 x 42" inner and middle border strips

From **BEIGE FLORAL**:
- Cut 4, 6-7/8" squares
- Cut 7, 6-1/2 x 42" middle border strips

From **LIGHT GREEN PRINT**:
- Cut 4, 6-7/8" squares

From **GOLD STRIPE**:
- Cut 9, 2-1/2 x 42" middle border strips

From **RED WILD ROSE**:
- Cut 4, 6-1/2" corner squares
- Cut 11, 6-1/2 x 42" outer border strips

Assembling and Attaching the Borders

Step 1 Attach the 2-1/2" wide **DARK GREEN PRINT** inner border strips.

Step 2 With right sides together, layer the 6-7/8" **BEIGE FLORAL** and **LIGHT GREEN PRINT** squares together in pairs. Press together, but do not sew. Cut the layered squares in half diagonally to make 8 sets of triangles. Stitch 1/4" from the diagonal edge of each pair of triangles; press. <u>At this point each triangle-pieced square should measure 6-1/2" square</u>.

Make 8, 6-1/2" triangle-pieced square blocks

Step 3 Measure your quilt from left to right through the middle including seam allowances. Subtract 12" from this measurement to allow for the triangle-pieced squares. Cut 2, 6-1/2" wide **BEIGE FLORAL** middle border strips to this measurement. Sew the triangle-pieced squares to the ends of both strips; press. Sew the border strips to the top and bottom edges of the quilt center; press.

Step 4 Measure your quilt from top to bottom through the middle including the seam allowances and the borders just added. Subtract 24" from this measurement to allow for the triangle-pieced squares and the 6-1/2" square **RED WILD ROSE** corner squares. Cut 2, 6-1/2" wide **BEIGE FLORAL** middle border strips to this measurement. Sew the triangle-pieced squares and **RED WILD ROSE** corner

squares to the ends of both strips; press. Sew the border strips to the side edges of the quilt center; press.

Step 5 Attach the 2-1/2" wide **DARK GREEN PRINT** middle border strips.

Step 6 Attach the 2-1/2" wide **GOLD STRIPE** middle border strips.

Step 7 Attach the 6-1/2" wide **RED WILD ROSE** outer border strips.

Putting It All Together

Cut the 8 yard length of backing fabric in thirds crosswise to make 3, 2-2/3 yard lengths. Refer to Finishing the Quilt on page 126 for complete instructions.

Binding
Cutting
From **DARK GREEN PRINT**:

- Cut 11, 6-1/2 x 42" strips

Sew the binding to the quilt using a scant 1" seam allowance. This measurement will produce a 1" wide finished double binding. Refer to Binding and Diagonal Piecing on page 127 for complete instructions.

Flannel Reflections

Fabrics and Supplies

for one Pillow Sham

1/3 yard	**RED PLAID** for pillow top
1-1/4 yards	**GOLD STRIPE** for prairie points and pillow ruffle
1/8 yard	**GREEN PRINT** for band
1-7/8 yards	**RED PRINT** for pillow top and back

6—1/2" diameter buttons

Quilting thread or pearl cotton for gathering ruffle

Bed pillow form (20 x 29")

Cutting

From **RED PLAID**:
- Cut 1, 8-3/4 x 21" pillow top rectangle

From **GOLD STRIPE**:
- Cut 6, 6-1/2 x 42" ruffle strips

- Cut 1, 4-1/2 x 42" strip. From this strip cut: 6, 4-1/2" squares for prairie points

From **GREEN PRINT**:
- Cut 1, 2-1/2 x 21" strip for band

From **RED PRINT**:
- Cut 2, 21 x 36" pillow back rectangles
- Cut 1, 19-3/4 x 21" pillow top rectangle

Prairie Points and Assemble the Pillow Top

Step 1 Fold a 4-1/2" **GOLD STRIPE** square in half diagonally with wrong sides together and press. Fold in half again and press. Repeat with the remaining squares to make 6 prairie points.

 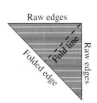

Step 2 With right sides together and aligning raw edges, position the prairie points along the long edge of the 8-3/4 x 21" **RED PLAID** rectangle. Starting at the left edge, overlap the ends of the prairie points. The corner tips of the end prairie points should be even with the side edges of the **RED PLAID** rectangle. Pin the prairie points in place and machine-baste them to the rectangle.

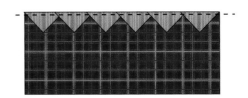

Step 3 Aligning raw edges, position the 2-1/2 x 21" **GREEN PRINT** band on the Step 2 Red Plaid rectangle with the prairie points sandwiched in between. Stitch the band in place and press the seam allowances toward the band.

Step 4 Aligning raw edges, stitch the 19-3/4 x 21" **RED PRINT** rectangle to the Step 3 unit. Press the seam allowance toward the band. <u>At this point the pillow top should measure 21 x 30".</u>

Step 5 Center a button on each prairie point and stitch in place.

Attach the Ruffle

Step 1 Diagonally piece together the 6-1/2" wide **GOLD STRIPE** ruffle strips to make a continuous ruffle strip, referring to Diagonal Piecing on page 125.

Step 2 Fold the strip in half lengthwise, wrong sides together, and press. Divide the ruffle strip into 4 equal segments, and mark the quarter points with safety pins.

Step 3 To gather the ruffle, position quilting thread (or pearl cotton) 1/4" from the raw edges of the folded ruffle strip. You will need a length of thread 200" long. Secure one end of the thread by stitching across it. Zigzag stitch over the thread all the way around the ruffle strip, taking care not to sew through it.

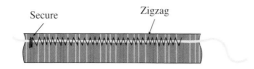

Secure   Zigzag

Step 4 Divide the edges of the pillow front into 4 equal segments and mark the quarter points with safety pins. With right sides together and raw edges aligned, pin the ruffle to the

pillow top, matching the quarter points. Pull up the gathering stitches until the ruffle fits the pillow front, taking care to allow extra fullness in the ruffle at each corner. Sew the ruffle to the pillow front, using a 1/4" seam allowance.

Assembling the Pillow Back

Step 1 With wrong sides together, fold each 21 x 36" **RED PRINT** pillow back rectangle in half crosswise to form 2, 18 x 21" double-thick pillow back pieces. Overlap the 2 folded edges so the pillow back measures 21 x 30". Pin the pieces together and stitch around the entire piece to create a single pillow back, using a scant 1/4" seam allowance.

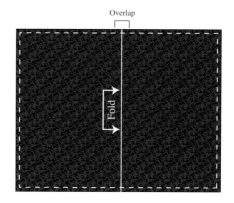

Overlap

Fold

Step 2 With right sides together, layer the pillow back and the pillow front, and pin. The ruffle will be sandwiched between the 2 layers and turned toward the center of the pillow at this time. Pin and stitch around the outside edges using a 1/2" seam allowance. Turn the pillow sham right side out, insert the pillow form through the pillow back opening, and fluff up the ruffle.

Flannel Reflections Dust Ruffle

Mattress: 52 x 75" with a 19" drop

Fabrics and Supplies

7-3/8 yards **BEIGE PLAID** for dust ruffle
(cut on the lengthwise grain)

2-1/8 yards **GOLD STRIPE** for trim band
(cut on the crosswise grain)

3-1/4 yards **MUSLIN** for center panel

Quilting thread or pearl cotton for gathering
dust ruffle

Special Measuring Instructions

If your drop length differs from 19", use the fol-
lowing instructions to determine the correct drop
length of your dust ruffle.

Step 1 Measure from the top edge of the box
spring to the floor, and add 2-1/2" to allow
for a hem and seam allowance.

Step 2 For ease in construction, make the dust
ruffle in 3 sections - 2 for the sides and
one for the foot end. To determine the
number of fabric strips to cut for the dust
ruffle, measure the side of your box spring
and multiply this length by 2 or 2-1/2,
depending on the fullness you want and
the weight of your fabric. Repeat for the
other side and the foot end of the bed.
Add these measurements together to get
the total inches needed.

Step 3 Cut and piece the strips of fabric
according to the measurements determined
in Steps 1 and 2.

Center Panel

Cut the 3-1/4 yard length of muslin in half crosswise to make 2, 1-5/8 yard lengths. Sew the long edges together; press. Trim the muslin to 53 x 79-1/2".

Note: If your mattress size differs from 52 x 75", measure the width and length of the bed's box spring. Add 1" to the width measurement to allow for 1/2" seam allowances at the side edges. Add 4-1/2" to the length measurement to allow for a double 2" hem at the top edge and a 1/2" seam allowance at the bottom edge. Cut a piece of muslin according to this measurement to make the center panel.

Preparing the Center Panel

Step 1 Turn the top edge of the muslin under 2"; press. Turn the same edge under another 2"; press. Edge-stitch the folded edgein place to hem the top edge of the center panel.

Step 2 Measure the side of the center panel, from point A to point B. Divide the measurement by 4 and mark those points on the side raw edges of the center panel with safety pins. Repeat for the other side (point C to point D) and the foot end (point B to point C).

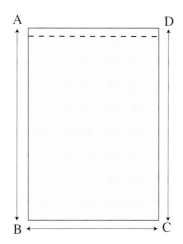

Make the Dust Ruffle

Note: For ease in construction, make the dust ruffle in 3 sections - 2 for the side ruffles and 1 for the bottom ruffle.

Cutting

From BEIGE PLAID
(cut on the lengthwise grain)
- Cut 2, 16-3/4 x 153" strips - for side ruffles
- Cut 1, 16-3/4 x 107" strip - for bottom ruffle

From GOLD STRIPE
(cut on the crosswise grain)
- Cut 11, 6-1/2 x 42" strips for band. Diagonally piece these strips together. From this strip cut:
  2, 6-1/2 x 153" strips - for side ruffles
  1, 6-1/2 x 107" strip - for bottom ruffle

Piecing

Step 1 To prepare the bottom edge band, fold the 6-1/2 x 107" **GOLD STRIPE** strip in half lengthwise with wrong sides together; press. At this point the **GOLD STRIPE** strip should measure 3-1/4 x 107". With right sides together and long raw edges aligned, sew the **GOLD STRIPE** strip to the 16-3/4 x 107" **BEIGE PLAID** strip using a 1/4" seam allowance. Press the seam allowances toward the **BEIGE PLAID** strip. At this point the pieced strip should measure 19-1/2 x 107".

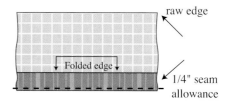

raw edge

Folded edge

1/4" seam allowance

Step 2 To hem the side edges of the pieced strip, turn one side edge under 1"; press. Turn the same edge under another 1", press, and edge-stitch the folded edge in place.

Repeat for the other side edge. Divide the top edge of the dust ruffle into four equal segments and mark with safety pins.

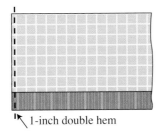

1-inch double hem

Step 3 To gather the dust ruffle, position 2 strands of quilting thread 1/4" from the raw edge. The length of thread should be the length of the dust ruffle strip. Referring to the gathering diagram below, secure one end of double thread by stitching across it. Zigzag-stitch over the thread, pushing the fabric onto the thread as you continue stitching.

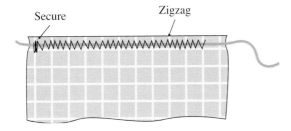

Secure   Zigzag

Step 4 With right sides together and raw edges aligned, pin the dust ruffle strip on the center panel matching the quarter points. Pull up the gathering threads to distribute the fullness of the ruffle evenly within each of the four sections. Pin the ruffle in place and stitch together using a 1/2" seam allowance.

Step 5 To prepare the dust ruffle for the side edges, fold the 6-1/2 x 153" **GOLD STRIPE** strips in half lengthwise with wrong sides together and press. With right sides together and long raw edges aligned, sew the 3-1/2" wide **GOLD STRIPE** strips to the 16-3/4 x 153" **BEIGE PLAID** strip using a 1/4" seam allowance, and press. <u>At this point each pieced strip should measure 19-1/2 x 153"</u>. Repeat Steps 2, 3, and 4 to hem, gather, and sew the dust ruffle strips to the side edges of the center panel.

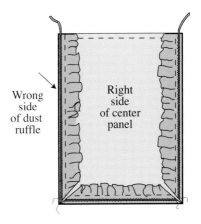

Wrong side of dust ruffle

Right side of center panel

Hourglass Flannel Patches

Finished Size: 74 x 86"   **Block: 6" square**

Fabrics and Supplies

3/4 yard	**BLUE CHECK** for triangle blocks
3/4 yard	**RED PRINT #1** for triangle blocks
3/4 yard	**BLUE FLORAL** for triangle blocks
3/4 yard	**GOLD STRIPE** for triangle blocks
1/2 yard	**BLUE MITTEN PRINT** for quilt center squares
1/2 yard	**GOLD DIAGONAL PRINT** for quilt center squares
1/4 yard	**BLUE PLAID** for quilt center squares
1/4 yard	**RED PRINT #2** for quilt center squares
1/4 yard	**MEDIUM GOLD PRINT** for quilt center squares
1/4 yard	**DARK BLUE PRINT** for quilt center squares
7/8 yard	**DARK GOLD PRINT** for inner border
2-7/8 yards	**RED PLAID** for quilt center squares and outer border (cut on the lengthwise grain)
1-2/3 yards	**DARK BLUE PRINT** for binding
5-1/4 yards	backing fabric

quilt batting, at least 78 x 90"

Triangle Blocks

Make 50 blocks

Cutting

From **BLUE CHECK, RED PRINT #1, BLUE FLORAL,** and **GOLD STRIPE:**

- Cut 3, 7-1/4 x 42" strips from each fabric. From the strips cut:
  13, 7-1/4" squares. Cut the squares diagonally into quarters, to make 52 triangles.

You will be using only 50 triangles from each fabric.

Piecing

Step 1 Layer a **BLUE CHECK** triangle on a **RED PRINT #1** triangle. Stitch along the bias edge; press. Repeat with the remaining **BLUE CHECK** and **RED PRINT #1** triangles, stitching along the same bias edge of each triangle set.

Bias edges

Make 50

Step 2 Layer a **BLUE FLORAL** triangle on a **GOLD STRIPE** triangle. Stitch along the bias edge; press. Repeat with the remaining **BLUE FLORAL** and **GOLD STRIPE** triangles, stitching along the same bias edge of each triangle set.

Bias edges

Make 50

Step 3 Sew together the Step 1 and Step 2 triangle units in pairs; press. <u>At this point each triangle block should measure 6-1/2" square.</u>

Make 50 triangle blocks

Quilt Center

Cutting

From **BLUE MITTEN PRINT**:
- Cut 2, 6-1/2 x 42" strips. From the strips cut: 10, 6-1/2" squares

From **GOLD DIAGONAL PRINT**:
- Cut 2, 6-1/2 x 42" strips. From the strips cut: 12, 6-1/2" squares

From **RED PRINT #2** and **DARK BLUE PRINT**:
- Cut 1, 6-1/2 x 42" strip from each fabric. From the strips cut:
  6, 6-1/2" squares from each fabric

From **BLUE PLAID, MEDIUM GOLD PRINT** and **RED PLAID**:
- Cut 1, 6-1/2 x 42" strip from each fabric. From the strips cut:
  5, 6-1/2" squares from each fabric

Quilt Center Assembly

Step 1 Referring to the quilt diagram for color placement, sew together the triangle blocks and the 6-1/2" quilt center squares in 9 vertical rows. Press the seam allowances toward the quilt center squares so the seams will fit together snugly with less bulk. At this point each block row should measure 6-1/2 x 66-1/2".

Note: The block rows must all be the same length. Adjust the seam allowances if needed.

Step 2 Pin the block rows together at the block intersections and sew the rows together. Press the seam allowances in one direction.

Borders

Note: The yardage given allows for the RED PLAID outer border strips to be cut on the lengthwise grain (a couple extra inches are allowed for trimming). Cutting the strips on the lengthwise grain will eliminate the need for piecing and matching the plaid. The yardage given allows for the DARK GOLD inner border strips to be cut on the crosswise grain.

Diagonally piece the strips as needed, referring to Diagonal Piecing instructions on page 125. Read through Border instructions on page 125 for general instructions on adding borders.

Cutting

From **DARK GOLD PRINT**:
- Cut 8, 2-1/2 x 42" inner border strips

From **RED PLAID**:
- Cut 2, 8-1/2 x 90" side outer border strips
- Cut 2, 8-1/2 x 60" top/bottom outer border strips

Attaching the Borders

Step 1 Attach the 2-1/2" wide **DARK GOLD PRINT** inner border strips.

Step 2 Attach the 8-1/2" wide **RED PLAID** outer border strips.

Putting It All Together

Cut the 5-1/4 yard length of backing fabric in half crosswise to make 2, 2-5/8 yard lengths. Refer to Finishing the Quilt on page 126 for complete instructions.

Binding

Cutting

From **DARK BLUE PRINT**:
- Cut 9, 6-1/2 x 42" strips

Sew the binding to the quilt using a scant 1" seam allowance. This measurement will produce a 1" wide finished double binding. Refer to Binding and Diagonal Piecing on page 127 for complete instructions.

Hourglass Flannel Patches

Ring Toss

Finished Size: 80 x 98"   *Block: 16" square*

Fabrics and Supplies

1/3 yard	**RED PLAID** for center squares
1 yard	**TAN PRINT** for blocks
3-1/4 yards	**BROWN PRINT** for blocks and outer border
1-7/8 yards	**GREEN PRINT** for blocks
2-1/8 yards	**RED LEAF PRINT** for blocks, lattice and inner border strips, nine patch corner squares, and pieced border
1-3/8 yards	**BEIGE PRINT** for pieced border and nine patch corner squares
1-7/8 yards	**GREEN PRINT** for binding
7-1/8 yards	backing fabric

quilt batting, at least 84 x 102"

Pieced Blocks

Make 12 blocks

Cutting

From RED PLAID:
- Cut 2, 4-1/2 x 42" strips. From the strips cut:
  12, 4-1/2" squares

From TAN PRINT:
- Cut 2, 1-1/2 x 42" strips. From the strips cut:
  48, 1-1/2" squares

- Cut 9, 2-1/2 x 42" strips. From the strips cut:
  24, 2-1/2 x 8-1/2" rectangles
  24, 2-1/2 x 4-1/2" rectangles

From BROWN PRINT:
- Cut 17, 2-1/2 x 42" strips. From the strips cut:
  24, 2-1/2 x 12-1/2" rectangles
  24, 2-1/2 x 8-1/2" rectangles
  48, 2-1/2" squares

From GREEN PRINT:
- Cut 23, 2-1/2 x 42" strips. From the strips cut:
  24, 2-1/2 x 16-1/2" rectangles
  24, 2-1/2 x 12-1/2" rectangles
  48, 2-1/2" squares

From RED LEAF PRINT:
- Cut 3, 2-1/2 x 42" strips. From the strips cut:
  48, 2-1/2" squares

Piecing

Step 1 Position 1-1/2" **TAN PRINT** squares on the corners of a 4-1/2" **RED PLAID** square. Draw a diagonal line on the **TAN PRINT** squares, and stitch on the line. Trim the seam allowances to 1/4"; press.

Make 12

Step 2 Sew 2-1/2 x 4-1/2" **TAN PRINT** rectangles to the top/bottom edges of the Step 1 unit; press. Sew 2-1/2 x 8-1/2" **TAN PRINT** rectangles to the side edges of this unit;

press. Position 2-1/2" **BROWN PRINT** squares on the corners of the unit. Draw a diagonal line on the **BROWN PRINT** squares, stitch, trim, and press.

Make 12

Step 3 Sew 2-1/2 x 8-1/2" **BROWN PRINT** rectangles to the top/bottom edges of the Step 2 unit; press. Sew 2-1/2 x 12-1/2" **BROWN PRINT** rectangles to the side edges of the unit; press. Position 2-1/2" **GREEN PRINT** squares on the corners of the unit. Draw a diagonal line on the **GREEN** squares, stitch, trim, and press.

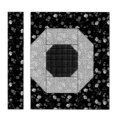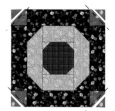

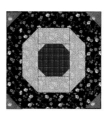

Make 12

Step 4 Sew 2-1/2 x 12-1/2" **GREEN PRINT** rectangles to the top/bottom edges of the Step 3 unit; press. Sew 2-1/2 x 16-1/2" **GREEN PRINT** rectangles to the side edges of the unit; press. Position 2-1/2" **RED LEAF PRINT** squares on the corners of the unit. Draw a diagonal line on the **RED LEAF PRINT** squares, stitch, trim, and press. <u>At this point each block should measure 16-1/2" square.</u>

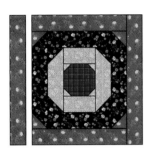 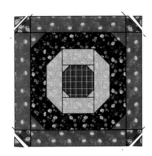

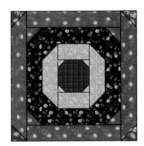

Make 12

Quilt Center

Note: The yardage given allows for the lattice and inner border strips to be cut on the crosswise grain. Diagonally piece the strips as needed, referring to Diagonal Piecing instructions on page 125.

Cutting

From **RED LEAF PRINT**:
- Cut 15, 2-1/2 x 42" strips. From the strips cut:
  8, 2-1/2 x 16-1/2" lattice strips
  5, 2-1/2 x 52-1/2" lattice/top and bottom inner border strips
  2, 2-1/2 x 74-1/2" side inner border strips

Quilt Center Assembly

Step 1 Referring to the quilt diagram, sew together 3 pieced blocks and 2, 2-1/2 x 16-1/2" **RED LEAF PRINT** lattice strips; press. Make 4 block rows.

Step 2 Referring to the quilt diagram, sew together the 4 block rows and 5, 2-1/2 x 52-1/2" **RED LEAF PRINT** lattice/top and bottom inner border strips; press.

Step 3 Sew the 2-1/2 x 74-1/2" **RED LEAF PRINT** inner border strips to the side edges of the quilt center; press.

Borders

Note: The yardage given allows for the border strips to be cut on the crosswise grain. Diagonally piece the strips as needed, referring to Diagonal Piecing instructions on page 125. Read through Border instructions on page 125 for General Instructions on adding borders.

Cutting

From **BEIGE PRINT**:
- Cut 14, 2-1/2 x 42" strips for the pieced border

- Cut 2 more 2-1/2 x 42" strips.
  From the strips cut:
  1, 2-1/2 x 22" strip for the nine patch corner squares
  2, 2-1/2 x 12" strips for the nine patch corner squares

From **RED LEAF PRINT**:
- Cut 7, 2-1/2 x 42" strips for the pieced border

- Cut 2 more 2-1/2 x 42" strips.
  From the strips cut:
  2, 2-1/2 x 22" strips for the nine patch corner squares
  1, 2-1/2 x 12" strip for the nine patch corner squares

From **BROWN PRINT**:
- Cut 10, 6-1/2 x 42" outer border strips

Piecing the Nine Patch Corner Squares

Note: The pieced border and nine patch corner squares are made up of strip sets. Refer to Hints and Helps for Pressing Strip Sets on page 122.

Step 1 Aligning long edges, sew a 2-1/2 x 22" **RED LEAF PRINT** strip to both side edges of a 2-1/2 x 22" **BEIGE PRINT** strip; press. Cut the strip set into segments.

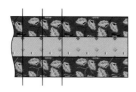

Crosscut 8, 2-1/2" wide segments

Step 2 Aligning long edges, sew a 2-1/2 x 12" **BEIGE PRINT** strip to both side edges of a 2-1/2 x 12" **RED LEAF PRINT** strip; press. Cut the strip set into segments.

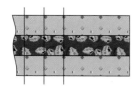

Crosscut 4, 2-1/2" wide segments

Step 3 For the nine patch corner squares, sew a Step 1 segment to both side edges of the Step 2 segments; press. At this point each nine patch corner square should measure 6-1/2" square.

Make 4

Attaching the Borders

Step 1 Diagonally piece together 7, 2-1/2 x 42" **BEIGE PRINT** strips; press. Repeat with the remaining 7, 2-1/2 x 42" **BEIGE PRINT** strips; press.

Step 2 Diagonally piece together 7, 2-1/2 x 42" **RED LEAF PRINT** strips; press.

Step 3 Aligning long edges, sew the 2-1/2" wide **BEIGE PRINT** strips to both side edges of the 2-1/2" wide **RED LEAF PRINT** strip; press. Treat the pieced border as one border strip.

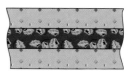

Pieced border

Step 4 To attach the pieced border strips with nine patch corner squares, refer to Borders with Corner Squares on page 126.

Step 5 Attach the 6-1/2" wide **BROWN PRINT** outer border strips.

Putting It All Together

Cut the 7-1/8 yard length of backing fabric in thirds crosswise to make 3, 2-3/8 yard lengths. Refer to Finishing the Quilt on page 126 for complete instructions.

Binding

Cutting

From **GREEN PRINT**:
• Cut 10, 6-1/2 x 42" strips

Sew the binding to the quilt using a scant 1" seam allowance. This measurement will produce a 1" wide finished double binding. Refer to Binding and Diagonal Piecing on page 127 for complete instructions.

Ring Toss

Snail's Trail

Finished Size: 80 x 104"   Block: 12" square

Fabrics and Supplies

1 yard each **12 ASSORTED PRINTS**
(PRINT #1, #2, #3, #4) for blocks

7/8 yard each **RED PRINT** and **BROWN FLORAL** for pieced border

1/4 yard **BROWN PRINT** for corner squares

2 yards **BROWN/BLACK PLAID**
for binding (cut on the bias)

7-1/8 yards backing fabric

quilt batting, at least 84 x 108"

Blocks A, B, and C

Make 16 blocks each of Block A, B, and C for a total
of 48 blocks

*Note: Divide your 12 ASSORTED PRINT FABRICS into 3 groups to
make Blocks A, B, and C. Each block will be using 4 different prints. Label
the prints in each group 1 through 4. We suggest cutting the fabric for one set
of blocks at a time to guard against mixing up the fabrics from block to block.
Label the blocks A, B, or C.*

Cutting

From each **PRINT #1**:
- Cut 6, 3-1/2 x 42" strips. From the strips cut:
  16, 3-1/2 x 9-1/2" rectangles
  16, 3-1/2" squares

- Cut 2 more 3-1/2 x 42" strips

From each **PRINT #2**:
- Cut 6, 3-1/2 x 42" strips. From the strips cut:
  32, 3-1/2 x 6-1/2" rectangles

- Cut 2 more 3-1/2 x 42" strips

From each **PRINT #3**:
- Cut 6, 3-1/2 x 42" strips. From the strips cut:
  16, 3-1/2 x 9-1/2" rectangles
  16, 3-1/2" squares

- Cut 2 more 3-1/2 x 42" strips

From each **PRINT #4**:
- Cut 6, 3-1/2 x 42" strips. From the strips cut:
  32, 3-1/2 x 6-1/2" rectangles

- Cut 2 more 3-1/2 x 42" strips

Piecing

Step 1 Position a 3-1/2 x 9-1/2" **PRINT #1** rectangle on the right corner of a 3-1/2 x 6-1/2" **PRINT #4** rectangle. Draw a diagonal line on the **PRINT #1** rectangle, and stitch on the line. Trim the seam allowance to 1/4"; press. <u>At this point each unit should measure 3-1/2 x 12-1/2"</u>.

Make 16

Step 2 Aligning long edges, sew the 3-1/2 x 42" **PRINT #1** and **PRINT #4** strips together in pairs; press. Make 2 strip sets. Cut the strip sets into segments.

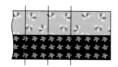

Crosscut 16, 3-1/2" wide segments

Step 3 Position a 3-1/2" **PRINT #1** square on the right corner of a 3-1/2 x 6-1/2" **PRINT #2** rectangle. Draw a diagonal line on the square, stitch, trim, and press.

Make 16

Step 4 Sew a Step 2 segment to the left edge of a Step 3 unit; press. <u>At this point each unit should measure 3-1/2 x 12-1/2"</u>.

Make 16

Step 5 Position a 3-1/2" **PRINT #3** square on the left edge of a 3-1/2 x 6-1/2" **PRINT #4** rectangle. Draw a diagonal line on the square, stitch, trim, and press.

Make 16

Step 6 Aligning long edges, sew the 3-1/2 x 42" **PRINT #2** and **PRINT #3** strips together in pairs; press. Make 2 strip sets. Cut the strip sets into segments.

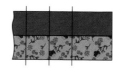

Crosscut 16, 3-1/2" wide segments

Step 7 Sew a Step 6 segment to the right edge of a Step 5 unit; press. <u>At this point each unit should measure 3-1/2 x 12-1/2"</u>.

Make 16

Step 8 Position a 3-1/2 x 6-1/2" **PRINT #2** rectangle on the right edge of a 3-1/2 x 9-1/2" **PRINT #3** rectangle. Draw a diagonal line on the **PRINT #2** rectangle, stitch, trim, and press. At this point each unit should measure 3-1/2 x 12-1/2".

Make 16

Step 9 Referring to the block diagram, sew the 4 horizontal units together; press. At this point each block should measure 12-1/2" square.

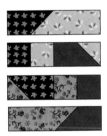 

Block A
Make 16

Step 10 Repeat Steps 1 through 9 using the remaining 2 groups of fabric to make 16 of Block B and 16 of Block C.

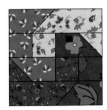 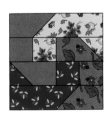

Block B
Make 16

Block C
Make 16

Quilt Center

Step 1 Referring to the quilt diagram for block placement, sew the A, B, and C blocks together in 8 rows of 6 blocks each. Press the seam allowances in alternating directions by rows so the seams will fit snugly together with less bulk.

Step 2 Pin the rows at the block intersections and sew the rows together. Press the seam allowances in one direction. At this point the quilt center should measure 72-1/2 x 96-1/2".

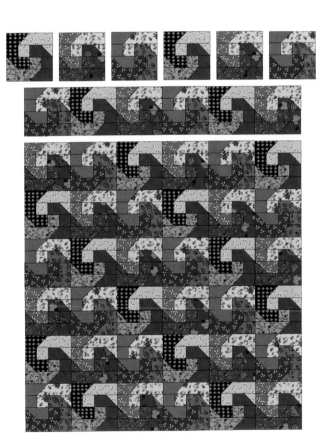

Pieced Border

Note: The yardage given allows for the border strips to be cut on the crosswise grain.

Cutting

From **RED PRINT** and **BROWN FLORAL**:
- Cut 5, 4-1/2 x 42" strips each.
  From the strips cut:
  14, 4-1/2 x 12-1/2" rectangles

From **BROWN PRINT**:
- Cut 4, 4-1/2" corner squares

Assembling and Attaching the Border

Step 1 For the top and bottom pieced borders, sew together 3 each of the 4-1/2 x 12-1/2" **RED PRINT** and **BROWN FLORAL** rectangles; press. Sew the pieced border strips to the quilt; press.

Step 2 For the side pieced borders, sew together 4 each of the 4-1/2 x 12-1/2" **RED PRINT** and **BROWN FLORAL** rectangles; press. Add the 4-1/2" **BROWN PRINT** corner squares to both ends of the border strips; press. Sew the pieced border strips to the quilt; press.

Putting It All Together

Cut the 7-1/8 yard length of backing fabric in thirds crosswise to make 3, 2-3/8 yard lengths. Refer to Finishing the Quilt on page 126 for complete instructions.

Binding

Cutting

From **BROWN/BLACK PLAID**:
- Cut enough 6-1/2" wide bias strips to make a 385" long strip

Sew the binding to the quilt using a scant 1" seam allowance. This measurement will produce a 1" wide finished double binding. Refer to Binding and Diagonal Piecing on page 127 for complete instructions.

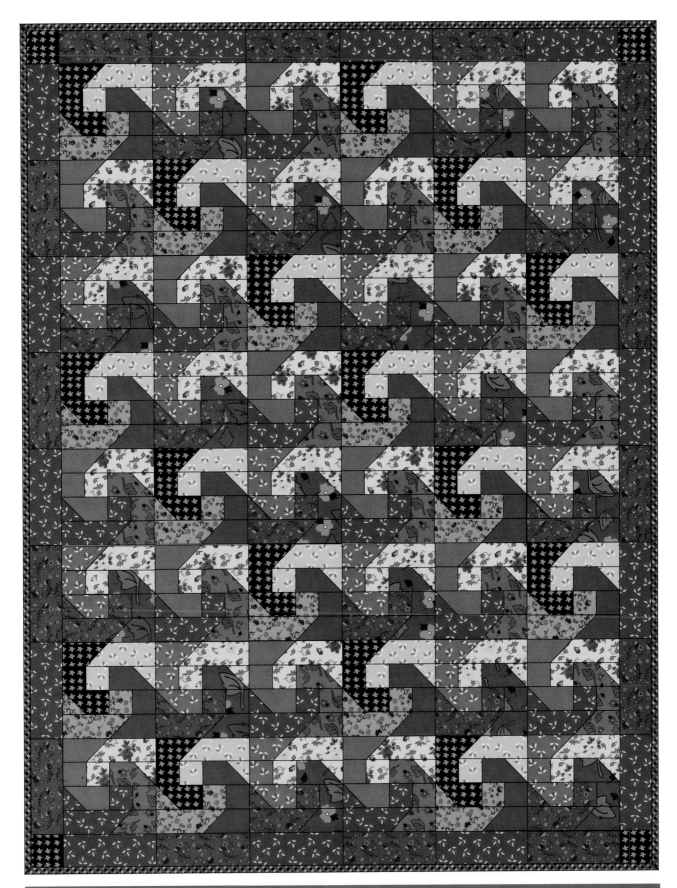

Snail's Trail

Crooked Path

Finished Size: 86 x 96"   *Block: 8" x 10"*

Fabrics and Supplies

1-1/2 yards	each of 4 **DARK PRINTS** for blocks
1-3/8 yards	each of 3 **BEIGE PRINTS** for background
1-1/2 yards	**GREEN FLORAL** for lattice and inner border
2 yards	**LARGE BLUE FLORAL** for outer border
1-2/3 yards	**CHESTNUT/RED PLAID** for binding (cut on the bias)
7-3/4 yards	backing fabric

quilt batting, at least 90 x 100"

Blocks

Make 60 blocks

Cutting

From each of the 4 **DARK PRINTS**:
- Cut 10, 4-1/2 x 42" strips. From the strips cut: 30, 4-1/2 x 10-1/2" rectangles

From each of the 3 **BEIGE PRINTS**:
- Cut 9, 4-1/2 x 42" strips. From the strips cut: 80, 4-1/2" squares

Piecing

Step 1 Position 4-1/2" **BEIGE PRINT** squares on the corners of a 4-1/2 x 10-1/2" **DARK PRINT** rectangle. Referring to the diagrams, draw a diagonal line on each square and stitch on the line. Trim the seam allowances to 1/4"; press.

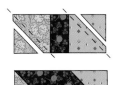

Make 60

Step 2 Position the remaining 4-1/2" **BEIGE PRINT** squares on the corners of the remaining 4-1/2 x 10-1/2" **DARK PRINT** rectangles. Referring to the diagrams, draw a diagonal line on the **BEIGE PRINT** squares in the opposite direction as you did for the Step 1 units and stitch, trim, and press.

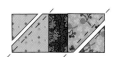

Make 60

Step 3 Sew together the Step 1 and 2 units in pairs; press. <u>At this point each block should measure 8-1/2 x 10-1/2"</u>.

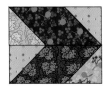

Make 60

Quilt Center

Note: The yardage given allows for the lattice and inner border strips to be cut on the crosswise grain. Diagonally piece the strips as needed, referring to Diagonal Piecing instructions on page 125.

Cutting

From GREEN FLORAL:
- Cut 18, 2-1/2 x 42" strips for lattice and inner border strips

Piecing

Step 1 Sew together 10 blocks to make a vertical block row. <u>At this point the block row should measure 10-1/2 x 80-1/2"</u>. Make 6 block rows.

Step 2 Cut 5, 2-1/2" wide **GREEN FLORAL** lattice strips 80-1/2" long or to the measurement of your block rows.

Step 3 Pin together the 6 block rows and the 5 **GREEN FLORAL** lattice strips. It is wise to place pins every 6" to secure the strips before sewing them together. This will prevent the flannel from moving and shifting. Sew the strips together; press.

Step 4 Attach the 2-1/2" wide **GREEN FLORAL** inner border strips.

Outer Border

Note: The yardage given allows for the border strips to be cut on the crosswise grain. Diagonally piece the strips as needed. Read through Border instructions on page 125 for general instructions on adding borders.

Cutting

From LARGE BLUE FLORAL:
- Cut 10, 6-1/2 x 42" outer border strips

Attaching the Outer Border

Attach the 6-1/2" wide **LARGE BLUE FLORAL** outer border strips.

Putting It All Together

Cut the 7-3/4 yard length of backing fabric into thirds crosswise to make 3, 2-5/8 yard lengths. Refer to Finishing the Quilt on page 126 for complete instructions.

Binding
Cutting
From **CHESTNUT/RED PLAID**:
- Cut enough 6-1/2" wide bias strips to make a 380" long strip

Sew the binding to the quilt using a scant 1" seam allowance. This measurement will produce a 1" wide finished double binding. Refer to Binding and Diagonal Piecing on page 127 for complete instructions.

Crooked Path

Sugar & Spice
Diamond Jubilee

Finished Size: 74 x 86"

2-1/8 yards **GREEN PRINT** for blocks,
middle border, and corner squares

1-1/2 yards **PURPLE PRINT** for blocks
and middle border

1-1/2 yards **GREEN LILY PRINT** for blocks
and inner border

3-1/3 yards **PURPLE WILD ROSE** for blocks
and outer border

2 yards **GREEN CHECK** for binding
(cut on the bias)

5-1/8 yards backing fabric

quilt batting, at least 78 x 90"

Triangle-Pieced Square Blocks

Cutting
From **GREEN PRINT**:
- Cut 3, 6-7/8 x 42" strips
- Cut 3 more 6-7/8 x 42" strips

From **PURPLE PRINT**:
- Cut 3, 6-7/8 x 42" strips
- Cut 1, 6-7/8 x 42" strip. From the strip cut:
  6, 6-7/8" squares

From **GREEN LILY PRINT**:
- Cut 2, 6-7/8 x 42" strips
- Cut 1, 6-7/8 x 42" strip. From the strip cut:
  4, 6-7/8" squares

From **PURPLE WILD ROSE**:
- Cut 3, 6-7/8 x 42" strips
- Cut 2 more 6-7/8 x 42" strips
- Cut 2, 6-7/8" squares

Piecing

Step 1 With right sides together, layer 3 of the
6-7/8 x 42" **GREEN PRINT** and **PURPLE
PRINT** strips together in pairs. Press
together, but do not sew. Cut the layered

strips into squares. Cut the layered squares
in half diagonally to make 32 sets of
triangles. Stitch 1/4" from the diagonal
edge of each pair of triangles; press. <u>At
this point each triangle-pieced square
block should measure 6-1/2" square.</u>

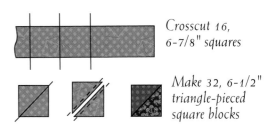

Crosscut 16,
6-7/8" squares

Make 32, 6-1/2"
triangle-pieced
square blocks

Step 2 Repeat the Step 1 process by layering 3 of
the 6-7/8 x 42" **PURPLE WILD ROSE**
and **GREEN PRINT** strips.

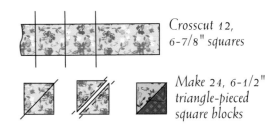

Crosscut 12,
6-7/8" squares

Make 24, 6-1/2"
triangle-pieced
square blocks

Step 3 Repeat the Step 1 process by layering 2 of
the 6-7/8 x 42" **PURPLE WILD ROSE**
and **GREEN LILY PRINT** strips.

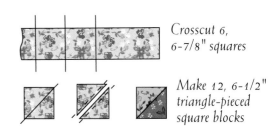

Crosscut 6,
6-7/8" squares

Make 12, 6-1/2"
triangle-pieced
square blocks

Step 4 With right sides together, layer 2 of the
6-7/8" **PURPLE PRINT** and **PURPLE
WILD ROSE** squares in pairs. Press
together, but do not sew. Cut the layered
squares in half diagonally to make 4 sets
of triangles; sew and press. <u>At this point</u>

each triangle-pieced square block should measure 6-1/2" square.

   Make 4, 6-1/2" triangle-pieced square blocks

Step 5 With right sides together, layer 4 of the 6-7/8" **GREEN LILY PRINT** and **PURPLE PRINT** squares in pairs. Press together, but do not sew. Cut the layered squares in half diagonally to make 4 sets of triangles; sew and press. <u>At this point each triangle-pieced square block should measure 6-1/2" square.</u>

   Make 8, 6-1/2" triangle-pieced square blocks

Quilt Center
Quilt Center Assembly

Step 1 Referring to the quilt assembly diagram for color placement, sew the triangle-pieced square blocks together in 10 rows of 8 blocks each. Press the seam allowances in alternating directions by rows so the seams will fit snugly together with less bulk.

Step 2 Pin the rows together at the block intersections and sew. Press the seam allowances in one direction. <u>At this point the quilt center should measure 48-1/2 x 60-1/2".</u>

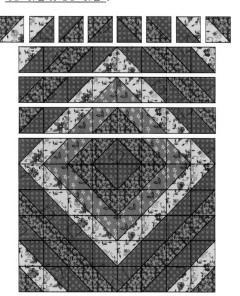

Borders

Note: The yardage given allows for the border strips to be cut on the crosswise grain. Diagonally piece the strips as needed, referring to Diagonal Piecing instructions on page 125. Read through Border instructions on page 125 for general instructions on adding borders.

Cutting

From **GREEN LILY PRINT**:
• Cut 7, 2-1/2 x 42" inner border strips

From **PURPLE PRINT**:
• Cut 7, 2-1/2 x 42" middle border strips

From **GREEN PRINT**:
• Cut 1, 7-1/2 x 42" strip. From the strip cut: 4, 7-1/2" corner squares
• Cut 7, 2-1/2 x 42" middle border strips

From **PURPLE WILD ROSE**:
• Cut 9, 7-1/2 x 42" outer border strips

Attaching the Borders

Step 1 Attach the 2-1/2" wide **GREEN LILY PRINT** inner border strips.

Step 2 Attach the 2-1/2" wide **PURPLE PRINT** middle border strips.

Step 3 Attach the 2-1/2" wide **GREEN PRINT** middle border strips.

Step 4 To attach the 7-1/2" wide **PURPLE WILD ROSE** outer border with **GREEN PRINT** corner squares, refer to Borders with Corner Squares on page 126.

Putting It All Together

Cut the 5 yard length of backing fabric in half crosswise to make 2, 2-1/2 yard lengths. Refer to Finishing the Quilt on page 126 for complete instructions.

Binding

Cutting

From GREEN CHECK:
- Cut enough 6-1/2" wide bias strips to make a 340" long strip

Sew the binding to the quilt using a scant 1" seam allowance. This measurement will produce a 1" wide finished double binding. Refer to Binding and Diagonal Piecing on page 127 for complete instructions.

Sugar & Spice Diamond Jubilee

Whisper Soft Pinwheels

Finished Size: 76 x 88"

Fabrics and Supplies

1-5/8 yards **BLACK FLORAL** for pinwheels

3/4 yard **BEIGE PRINT #1** for background

1-5/8 yards **BEIGE PRINT #2** for background

1-5/8 yards **BEIGE PRINT #3** for background

3/4 yard **GREEN PRINT** for inner border

2-3/4 yards **RED DIAGONAL PRINT** for outer border (cut on the lengthwise grain)

1-7/8 yards **TAN/RED PLAID** for binding (cut on the bias)

5-1/8 yards backing fabric

quilt batting, at least 80 x 92"

Blocks

Make 30 blocks

Cutting

From **BLACK FLORAL**:
- Cut 20, 2-1/2 x 42" strips. From the strips cut: 120, 2-1/2 x 6-1/2" rectangles

From **BEIGE PRINT #1**:
- Cut 8, 2-1/2 x 42" strips. From the strips cut: 120, 2-1/2" squares

From each of **BEIGE PRINT #2** and **#3**:
- Cut 20, 2-1/2 x 42" strips

Piecing

Step 1 Position a 2-1/2" **BEIGE PRINT** #1 square on the corner of a 2-1/2 x 6-1/2" **BLACK FLORAL** rectangle. Draw a diagonal line on the square and stitch on the line. Trim the seam allowance to 1/4"; press. <u>At this point each unit should measure 2-1/2 x 6-1/2"</u>.

Make 120

Step 2 Aligning long edges, sew the 2-1/2 x 42"
BEIGE PRINT #2 and **BEIGE PRINT #3**
strips together in pairs; press. Make 20
strip sets. Refer to page 122 for Hints and
Helps for Pressing Strip Sets. Cut the strip
sets into segments.

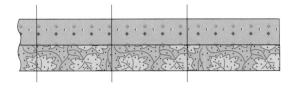

Crosscut 120, 6-1/2" wide segments

Step 3 Sew the Step 2 strip sets to the top edge of
the Step 1 units; press. <u>At this point each
unit should measure 6-1/2" square.</u>

Make 120

Step 4 Sew the Step 3 units together in pairs;
press. Sew the paired units together; press.
<u>At this point each block should measure
12-1/2" square.</u>

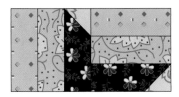

Make 60

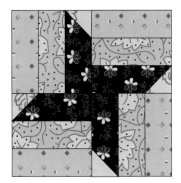

Make 30

Step 5 Referring to quilt diagram, sew 6 rows
of 5 pinwheel blocks each. Press the
seam allowances in alternating directions
by rows so the seams fit snugly together
with less bulk.

Step 6 Pin the rows at the block intersections and
sew the rows together. Press the seam
allowances in one direction.

Borders

*Note: The yardage given allows for the RED DIAGONAL
PRINT outer border strips to be cut on the lengthwise
grain (a couple extra inches are allowed for trimming).
Cutting the strips on the lengthwise grain will eliminate the
need for piecing and matching the print. The yardage given
allows for the GREEN PRINT inner strips to be cut on
the crosswise grain. Diagonally piece the strips as needed,
referring to Diagonal Piecing instructions on page 125.
Read through Border instructions on page 125 for general
instructions on adding borders.*

Cutting

From **GREEN PRINT**:
- Cut 8, 2-1/2 x 42" inner border strips

From **RED DIAGONAL PRINT**:
- Cut 2, 6-1/2 x 94" side outer border strips
  (cut on the lengthwise grain)

- Cut 2, 6-1/2 x 68" top/bottom outer border
  strips (cut on the lengthwise grain)

Attaching the Borders

Step 1 Attach the 2-1/2" wide **GREEN PRINT**
inner border strips.

Step 2 Attach the 6-1/2" wide **RED DIAGONAL
PRINT** outer border strips.

Putting It All Together

Cut the 5-1/8 yard length of backing fabric
in half crosswise to make 2, 2-5/8 yard lengths.
Refer to Finishing the Quilt on page 126 for
complete instructions.

Binding

Cutting

From **TAN/RED PLAID**:

- Cut enough 6-1/2" wide bias strips to make a 345" long strip

Sew the binding to the quilt using a scant 1" seam allowance. This measurement will produce a 1" wide finished double binding. Refer to Binding and Diagonal Piecing instructions on page 127 for complete instructions.

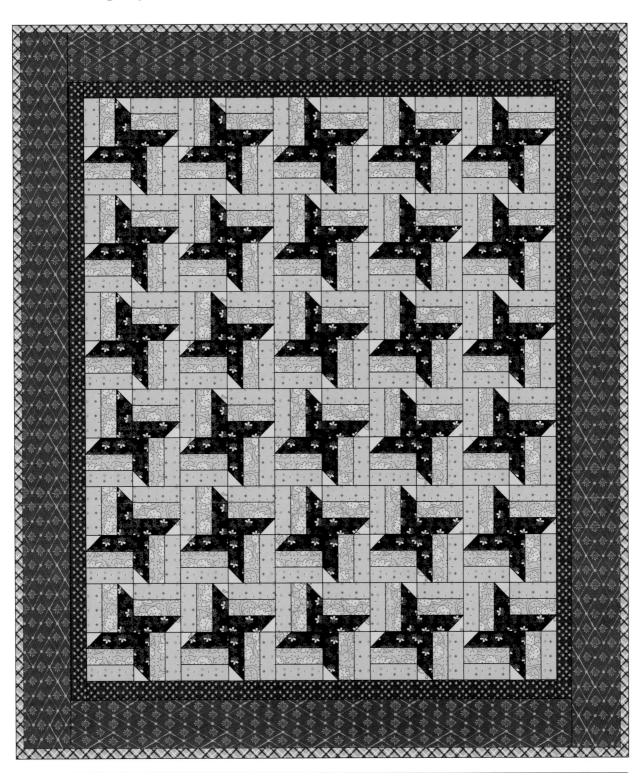

Whisper Soft Pinwheels

Stepping Stone

Finished Size: 83 x 103"   Block: 10" square

Fabrics and Supplies

3-1/2 yards **RED GRID** for blocks and outer border

1 yard **GREEN PRINT** for blocks

1-1/2 yards **LARGE GOLD FLORAL** for blocks

1-1/2 yards **GREEN FLORAL** for blocks

2-1/4 yards **RED PRINT** for blocks

3/4 yard **GOLD FLORAL** for inner border

2 yards **GREEN PRINT** for binding

7-1/2 yards backing fabric

quilt batting, at least 87 x 107"

Blocks

Make 48 blocks

Cutting

From **RED GRID**:
- Cut 5, 3-1/2 x 42" strips. From the strips cut: 48, 3-1/2" squares

From **GREEN PRINT**:
- Cut 3, 2-1/2 x 42" strips. From the strips cut: 48, 2-1/2" squares
- Cut 11, 1-1/2 x 42" strips

From **LARGE GOLD FLORAL**:
- Cut 3, 2-1/2 x 42" strips. From the strips cut: 48, 2-1/2" squares
- Cut 15 more 2-1/2 x 42" strips

From **GREEN FLORAL**:
- Cut 8, 2-1/2 x 42" strips. From the strips cut: 48, 2-1/2 x 6-1/2" rectangles
- Cut 9 more 2-1/2 x 42" strips

From **RED PRINT**:
- Cut 12, 2-1/2 x 42" strips. From the strips cut: 48, 2-1/2 x 8-1/2" rectangles
- Cut 12 more 2-1/2 x 42" strips

Piecing

Step 1 Sew a 1-1/2" wide **GREEN PRINT** strip to a 3-1/2" **RED GRID** square. Press the seam allowance toward the strip and trim the strip even with the edges of the square.

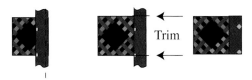

Step 2 Turn the unit to the left a quarter turn and sew a 1-1/2" wide **GREEN PRINT** strip to the unit; press and trim.

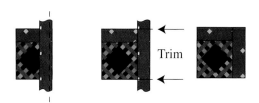

Step 3 Turn the unit to the right a quarter turn and sew a 2-1/2" wide **LARGE GOLD FLORAL** strip to the unit; press and trim.

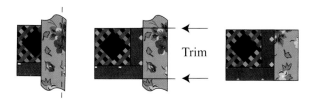

Step 4 Turn the unit to the left a quarter turn and sew a 2-1/2" wide **LARGE GOLD FLORAL** strip to the unit; press and trim.

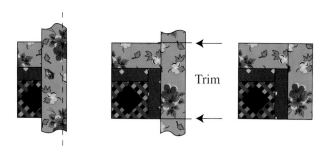

Step 5 Turn the unit to the right a quarter turn and sew a 2-1/2" wide **GREEN FLORAL** strip to the unit; press and trim.

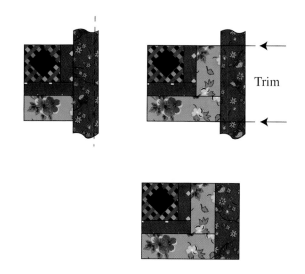

Step 6 Sew a 2-1/2" **LARGE GOLD FLORAL** square to a 2-1/2 x 6-1/2" **GREEN FLORAL** rectangle; press. Sew this unit to the Step 5 unit; press.

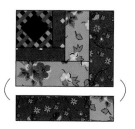

Step 7 Sew a 2-1/2" wide **RED PRINT** strip to the Step 6 unit; press and trim.

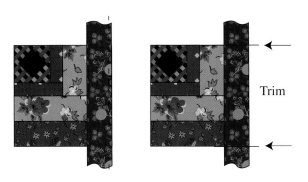

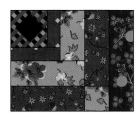

Step 8 Sew a 2-1/2" **GREEN PRINT** square to a 2-1/2 x 8-1/2" **RED PRINT** rectangle; press. Sew this unit to the Step 7 unit; press. <u>At this point each block should measure 10-1/2" square</u>.

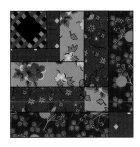

Make 48

Quilt Center

Note: Extra lattice strips are assembled to add to the top of the quilt center and to the right-hand side of the quilt center.

Cutting

From **RED PRINT**:
• Cut 4, 2-1/2 x 42" strips. From the strips cut: 14, 2-1/2 x 8-1/2" rectangles

From **GREEN PRINT**:
• Cut 1, 2-1/2 x 42" strip. From the strip cut: 15, 2-1/2" squares

Assembling the Quilt Center

Step 1 Referring to the quilt diagram for block placement, sew the blocks together in 8 rows of 6 blocks each. Press the seam allowances in alternating directions by rows so the seams will fit snugly together with less bulk.

Step 2 Pin the rows at the block intersections and sew the rows together. Press the seam allowances in one direction.

Step 3 For the top lattice strip, sew together 6 of the 2-1/2 x 8-1/2" **RED PRINT** rectangles and 6 of the 2-1/2" **GREEN PRINT** squares; press. Sew the lattice strip to the top of the quilt center; press.

Step 4 For the right-hand side lattice strip, sew together 8 of the 2-1/2 x 8-1/2" **RED PRINT** rectangles and 9 of the 2-1/2" **GREEN PRINT** squares; press. Sew the lattice strip to the quilt center; press.

Borders

Note: The yardage given allows for the border strips to be cut on the crosswise grain. Diagonally piece the strips as needed, referring to Diagonal Piecing instructions on page 125. Read through Border instructions on page 125 for general instructions on adding borders.

Cutting

From **GOLD FLORAL**:
• Cut 9, 2-1/2 x 42" inner border strips

From **RED GRID**:
• Cut 11, 9 x 42" outer border strips

Attaching the Borders

Step 1 Attach the 2-1/2" wide **GOLD FLORAL** inner border strips.

Step 2 Attach the 9" wide **RED GRID** outer border strips.

Putting It All Together

Cut the 7-1/2 yard length of backing fabric into thirds crosswise to make 3, 2-1/2 yard lengths. Refer to Finishing the Quilt on page 126 for complete instructions.

Binding

Cutting
From **GREEN PRINT**:

• Cut 10, 6-1/2 x 42" strips

Sew the binding to the quilt using a scant 1" seam allowance. This measurement will produce a 1" wide finished double binding. Refer to Binding and Diagonal Piecing on page 127 for complete instructions.

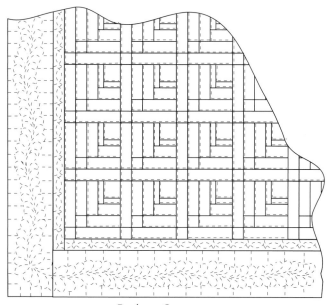

Quilting Suggestion

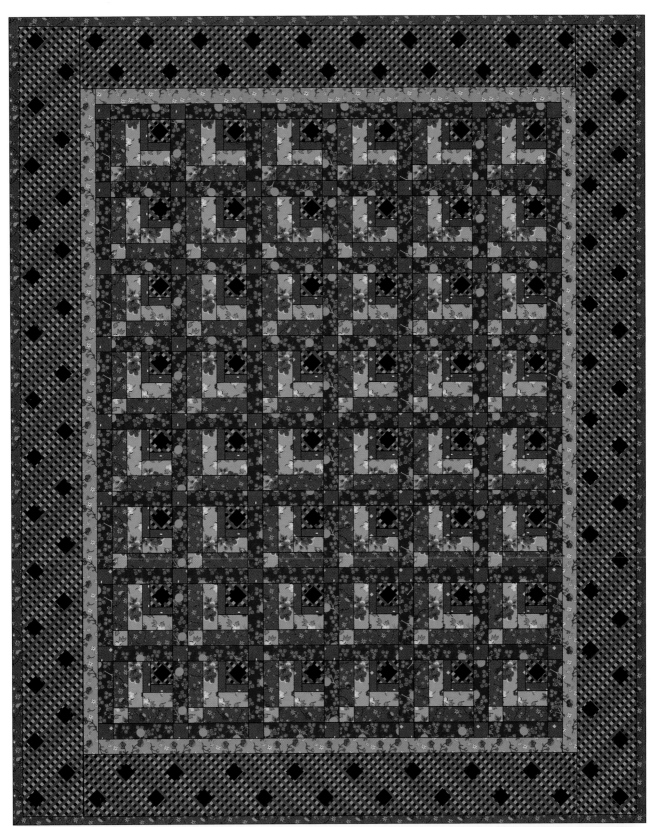

Stepping Stone

Block City

Finished Size: 48 x 60"   *Block: 10" square*

Fabrics and Supplies

1-1/4 yards **RED PRINT** for house blocks and lattice pieces

1/2 yard **MEDIUM GOLD PRINT** for house blocks and inner border

1/2 yard **BLACK PRINT** for house blocks and lattice posts

1/2 yard **BEIGE PRINT** for house blocks

1/3 yard **GREEN PRINT** for log cabin strips

3/8 yard **BLUE PRINT** for log cabin strips

3/4 yard **DARK GOLD PRINT** for log cabin strips

1 yard **GREEN FLORAL** for outer border

1-1/4 yards **BLACK PRINT** for binding

3 yards backing fabric

quilt batting, at least 52 x 64"

House Blocks

Make 12 blocks

Cutting

From **RED PRINT**:
- Cut 3, 2-1/2 x 42" strips. From the strips cut: 24, 2-1/2 x 3-1/2" rectangles

From **MEDIUM GOLD PRINT**:
- Cut 1, 3-1/2 x 42" strip. From the strip cut: 12, 2-1/2 x 3-1/2" rectangles

From **BLACK PRINT**:
- Cut 2, 3-1/2 x 42" strips. From the strips cut: 12, 3-1/2 x 6-1/2" rectangles

From **BEIGE PRINT**:
- Cut 3, 3-1/2 x 42" strips. From the strips cut: 24, 3-1/2" squares

From **GREEN PRINT**:
- Cut 4, 1-1/2 x 42" strips

From **BLUE PRINT**:
- Cut 6, 1-1/2 x 42" strips

From **DARK GOLD PRINT**:
- Cut 14, 1-1/2 x 42" strips

Piecing

Step 1 Position a 3-1/2" **BEIGE PRINT** square on the corner of a 3-1/2 x 6-1/2" **BLACK PRINT** rectangle. Draw a diagonal line on the square and stitch on the line. Trim the seam allowance to 1/4"; press. Repeat this process at the opposite corner of the rectangle.

Make 12

Step 2 Sew a 2-1/2 x 3-1/2" **RED PRINT** rectangle to both side edges of a 2-1/2 x 3-1/2" **MEDIUM GOLD PRINT** rectangle; press. Make 12 units. Sew the Step 1 roof units to the top edge of the house base units; press. <u>At this point each house block should measure 6-1/2" square.</u>

Make 12   *Make 12*

Step 3 Sew a 1-1/2" wide **GREEN PRINT** strip to the top/bottom edges of the house block. Press and trim each strip even with the house block.

Make 12

Step 4 Sew a 1-1/2" wide **BLUE PRINT** strip to the side edges of the house block; press and trim.

Step 5 Sew a 1-1/2" wide **DARK GOLD PRINT** strip to the top/bottom edges of the house block; press and trim. Sew a 1-1/2" wide **DARK GOLD PRINT** strip to the side edges of the house block; press and trim. At this point each house block should measure 10-1/2".

Make 12

Quilt Center

Cutting

From **RED PRINT**:
- Cut 11, 2-1/2 x 42" strips. From the strips cut: 31, 2-1/2 x 10-1/2" lattice pieces

From **BLACK PRINT**:
- Cut 2, 2-1/2 x 42" strips. From the strips cut: 20, 2-1/2" lattice post squares

Quilt Center Assembly

Step 1 Sew together 3 of the house blocks and 4 of the **RED PRINT** lattice pieces. Press the seam allowances toward the lattice pieces. Make 4 block rows. At this point each block row should measure 10-1/2 x 38-1/2".

Note: The block rows must all be the same length. Adjust the seam allowances if needed.

Step 2 Sew together 3 of the **RED PRINT** lattice pieces and 4 of the **BLACK PRINT** lattice post squares. Press the seam allowances toward the lattice pieces. Make 5 lattice

strips. At this point each lattice strip should measure 2-1/2 x 38-1/2".

Step 3 Referring to the quilt diagram, pin the block rows and lattice strips together; sew and press. At this point the quilt center should measure 38-1/2 x 50-1/2".

Borders

Note: The yardage given allows for the border strip to be cut on the crosswise grain. Diagonally piece the strips as needed, referring to Diagonal Piecing instructions on page 125. Read through Border instructions on page 125 for general instructions on adding borders.

Cutting

From **MEDIUM GOLD PRINT**:
- Cut 5, 1-1/2 x 42" inner border strips

From **GREEN FLORAL**:
- Cut 6, 4-1/2 x 42" outer border strips

Attaching the Borders

Step 1 Attach the 1-1/2" wide **MEDIUM GOLD PRINT** inner border strips.

Step 2 Attach the 4-1/2" wide **GREEN FLORAL** outer border strips.

Putting It All Together

Cut the 3 yard length of backing fabric in half crosswise to make 2, 1-1/2 yard lengths. Refer to Finishing the Quilt on page 126 for complete instructions.

Binding
Cutting
From **BLACK PRINT**:
- Cut 6, 6-1/2 x 42" strips

Sew the binding to the quilt using a scant 1" seam allowance. This measurement will produce a 1" wide finished double binding. Refer to Binding and Diagonal Piecing on page 127 for complete instructions.

Block City

Summer Night Tile Strippy

Finished Size: 70 x 84"

Fabrics and Supplies

1-3/8 yards **RED PRINT** for quilt center
and corner squares

1-1/2 yards **BEIGE PRINT** for quilt center

7/8 yard **GREEN TICKING** for quilt center
and inner border

3-1/8 yards **GREEN FLORAL** for vertical lattice
strips and outer border

1-7/8 yards **GREEN TICKING** for binding

5 yards backing fabric

quilt batting, at least 74 x 88"

Strip Pieced Vertical Strips

Note: The quilt center is made up of strip sets. Refer to Hints and Helps for Pressing Strip Sets on page 122.

Cutting

From **RED PRINT**:
 • Cut 13, 2-1/2 x 42" strips

From **BEIGE PRINT**:
 • Cut 18, 2-1/2 x 42" strips

From **GREEN TICKING**:
 • Cut 2, 2-1/2 x 42" strips

Piecing

Step 1 Aligning long edges, sew 2 of the 2-1/2 x 42" **BEIGE PRINT** strips to both side edges of a 2-1/2 x 42" **RED** strip. Press the seam allowances toward the **RED PRINT** strip. Make a total of 9 strip sets. Cut the strip sets into segments.

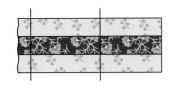

Crosscut 35, 8-1/2" wide segments

Step 2 Aligning long edges, sew 2 of the 2-1/2 x 42" red strips to both side edges of a 2-1/2 x 42" **GREEN TICKING** strip. Press the seam allowances toward the **RED PRINT** strips. Make a total of 2 strip sets. Cut the strip sets into segments.

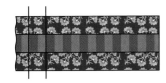

Crosscut 30, 2-1/2" wide segments

Step 3 Referring to the quilt diagram, sew 7 of the Step 1 segments and 6 of the Step 2 segments together in 5 vertical strips; press. <u>At this point each pieced vertical strip should measure 6-1/2 x 68-1/2"</u>.

Quilt Center and Borders

Note: The yardage given allows for the border strips to be cut on the crosswise grain. Diagonally piece the strips as needed, referring to Diagonal Piecing instructions on page 125. Read through Border instructions on page 125 for general instructions on adding borders.

Cutting

From **GREEN TICKING**:
- Cut 7, 2-1/2 x 42" inner border strips

From **GREEN FLORAL**:
- Cut 8, 6-1/2 x 42" vertical lattice strips
- Cut 8 more 6-1/2 x 42" outer border strips

From **RED PRINT**:
- Cut 1, 6-1/2 x 42" strip. From the strip cut: 4, 6-1/2" corner squares

Quilt Center Assembly

Diagonally piece the 6-1/2" wide **GREEN FLORAL** vertical lattice strips and cut them to 68-1/2" long (or the measurement of your pieced vertical rows). Pin together the 5 pieced vertical strips and the 4 **GREEN FLORAL** vertical lattice strips. Sew the strips together; press. <u>At this point the quilt center should measure 54-1/2 x 68-1/2"</u>.

Attaching the Borders

Step 1 Attach the 2-1/2" wide **GREEN TICKING** inner border strips.

Step 2 To attach the 6-1/2" wide **GREEN FLORAL** outer border strips with 6-1/2" **RED PRINT** corner squares, refer to Borders with Corner Squares on page 126.

Putting It All Together

Cut the 5 yard length of backing fabric in half crosswise to make 2, 2-1/2 yard lengths. Refer to Finishing the Quilt on page 126 for complete instructions.

Binding

Cutting

From **GREEN TICKING**:
- Cut 9, 6-1/2 x 42" strips

Sew the binding to the quilt using a scant 1" seam allowance. This measurement will produce a 1" wide finished double binding. Refer to Binding and Diagonal Piecing on page 127 for complete instructions.

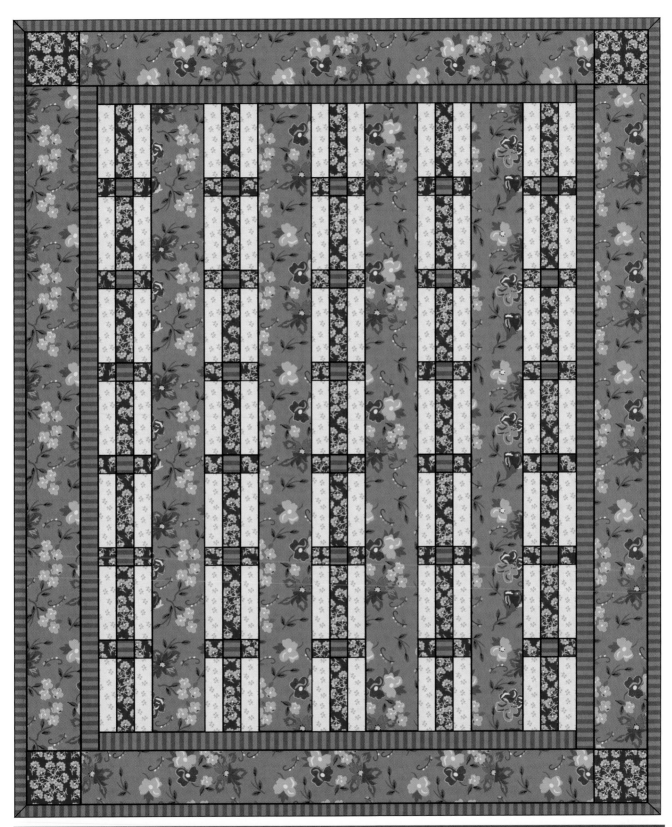

Summer Night Tile Strippy

Window Grid Throw

Finished Size: 62 x 78"   Block: 6" square

2-1/4 yards **GREEN FLORAL**
for blocks and outer border

1/2 yard **BEIGE PRINT #1** for triangle blocks

1/2 yard **BEIGE PRINT #2** for triangle blocks

1/2 yard **GREEN PRINT #1**
for triangle blocks

1/2 yard **GREEN PRINT #2**
for triangle blocks

3/4 yard **DARK RED PRINT** for lattice pieces
and side inner borders

3/4 yard **RED PRINT #1** for lattice strips
and top/bottom inner borders

3/8 yard **GREEN PRINT #3**
for checkerboard border

3/4 yard **BEIGE PRINT #3** for checkerboard
and second middle border

3/8 yard **RED PRINT #2** for first
middle border

1-5/8 yards **DARK RED PRINT** for binding

4-3/4 yards backing fabric

quilt batting, at least 66 x 84"

Note: Accuracy is a must for this pattern as you will be adding a pieced border.

Triangle Blocks

Make 21 blocks

Cutting

From BEIGE PRINT #1 and #2:
- Cut 2, 7-1/4 x 42" strips from each fabric. From the strips cut:
6, 7-1/4" squares. Cut the squares diagonally into quarters, to make 24 triangles. You will be using only 21 triangles of each fabric.

From GREEN PRINT #1 and #2:
- Cut 2, 7-1/4 x 42" strips from each fabric. From the strips cut:
6, 7-1/4" squares. Cut the squares diagonally into quarters, to make 24 triangles. You will be using only 21 triangles of each fabric.

Piecing

Step 1 Layer a **GREEN PRINT #1** triangle on a **BEIGE PRINT #1** triangle. Stitch along the bias edge; press. Repeat with the remaining **GREEN PRINT #1** and **BEIGE PRINT #1** triangles, stitching along the same bias edge of each triangle set.

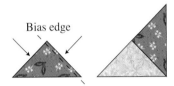

Bias edge

Make 21 triangle units

Step 2 Layer a **GREEN PRINT #2** triangle on a **BEIGE PRINT #2** triangle. Stitch along the bias edge; press. Repeat with the remaining **GREEN PRINT #2** and **BEIGE PRINT #2** triangles, stitching along the same bias edge of each triangle set.

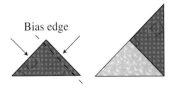

Bias edge

Make 21 triangle units

Step 3 Sew together the Step 1 and Step 2 triangle units in pairs; press. <u>At this point each triangle block should measure 6-1/2" square.</u>

Make 21 triangle blocks

Quilt Center

Cutting

From GREEN FLORAL:
- Cut 3, 6-1/2 x 42" strips. From the strips cut: 18, 6-1/2" squares for alternate blocks

From DARK RED PRINT:
- Cut 3, 2-1/2 x 42" side inner border strips. Diagonally piece the strips together.
- Cut 5, 2-1/2 x 42" strips. From the strips cut: 28, 2-1/2 x 6-1/2" rectangles for lattice pieces

From RED PRINT #1:
- Cut 8, 2-1/2 x 42" lattice and top/bottom inner border strips

Quilt Center Assembly

Step 1 Referring to the quilt diagram for block placement, sew together the triangle blocks, 6-1/2" **GREEN FLORAL** alternate blocks, and 2-1/2 x 6-1/2" **DARK RED PRINT** lattice pieces in 7 rows of 5 blocks each. Press the seam allowances toward the **DARK RED PRINT** lattice pieces. At this point each block row should measure 6-1/2 x 38-1/2".

Step 2 Cut the 8, 2-1/2" wide **RED PRINT #1** strips to 38-1/2" long or the measurement of your block rows. Pin together the 7 block rows and the 8 **RED PRINT #1** lattice strips. Sew the strips together; press.

Step 3 Attach the 2-1/2" wide **DARK RED PRINT** side inner border strips. At this point the quilt center should measure 42-1/2 x 58-1/2".

Borders

Note: The yardage given allows for the border strips to be cut on the crosswise grain. Diagonally piece the strips as needed, referring to Diagonal Piecing instructions on page 125. Read through Border instructions on page 125 for general instructions on adding borders. The checkerboard is made up of strip sets. Refer to Hints and Helps for Pressing Strip Sets on page 122.

Cutting

From GREEN PRINT #3:
- Cut 4, 2-1/2 x 42" strips for checkerboard border

From BEIGE PRINT #3:
- Cut 4, 2-1/2 x 42" strips for checkerboard border
- Cut 7, 1-1/2 x 42" second middle border strips

From RED PRINT #2:
- Cut 7, 1-1/2 x 42" first middle border strips

From GREEN FLORAL:
- Cut 8, 6-1/2 x 42" outer border strips

Piecing

Step 1 Aligning long edges, sew together the 2-1/2" wide **BEIGE PRINT #3** and **GREEN PRINT #3** strips in pairs; press. Make 4 strip sets. Cut the strip sets into segments.

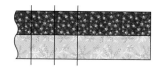

Crosscut 54, 2-1/2" wide segments

Step 2 For the top/bottom checkerboard borders, sew together 11 of the Step 1 segments. Remove one 2-1/2" **GREEN PRINT** square from the strip; press. At this point the top/bottom checkerboard borders should measure 2-1/2 x 42-1/2". Sew the checkerboard borders to the quilt center; press.

Step 3 For the side checkerboard borders, sew together 16 of the Step 1 segments. Remove one 2-1/2" **BEIGE PRINT** square from the strip; press. At this point the side checkerboard borders should measure 2-1/2 x 62-1/2". Sew the checkerboard borders to the quilt center; press.

Step 4 Attach the 1-1/2" wide **RED PRINT #2** first middle border strips.

Step 5 Attach the 1-1/2" wide **BEIGE PRINT #3** second middle border strips.

Step 6 Attach the 6-1/2" wide **GREEN FLORAL** outer border strips with triangle block corner squares. Refer to page 126 for Borders with Corner Squares.

Putting It All Together

Cut the 4-3/4 yard length of backing fabric in half crosswise to make 2, 2-3/8 yard lengths. Refer to Finishing the Quilt on page 126 for complete instructions.

Binding

Cutting

From **DARK RED PRINT**:
• Cut 8, 6-1/2 x 42" strips

Sew the binding to the quilt using a scant 1" seam allowance. This measurement will produce a 1" wide finished double binding. Refer to Binding and Diagonal Piecing on page 127 for complete instructions.

Window Grid Throw

Picnic Quilt

Finished Size: 64 x 76"

Fabrics and Supplies

1-1/8 yards **RED PRINT**
for flying geese blocks and bands

3 yards **MEDIUM GREEN PRINT** for flying geese background and outer border

1/2 yard **DARK GREEN PRINT**
for inner border

1 yard **RED FLORAL** for center rectangle and bands

1-2/3 yards **RED PRINT** for binding

4-1/2 yards backing fabric

quilt batting, at least 68 x 80"

Flying Geese Blocks

Make 20 blocks

Cutting

From **RED PRINT**:
- Cut 5, 4-1/2 x 42" strips. From the strips cut: 20, 4-1/2 x 8-1/2" rectangles
- Cut 4, 2-1/2 x 40-1/2" strips

From **MEDIUM GREEN PRINT**:
- Cut 5, 4-1/2 x 42" strips. From the strips cut: 40, 4-1/2" squares

Piecing

Step 1 Position a 4-1/2" **MEDIUM GREEN PRINT** square on the corner of a 4-1/2 x 8-1/2" **RED PRINT** rectangle. Draw a diagonal line on the square and stitch on the line. Trim the seam allowance to 1/4"; press. Repeat this process at the opposite corner of the rectangle. <u>At this point each flying geese block should measure 4-1/2 x 8-1/2"</u>.

Make 20

Step 2 Sew 10 of the flying geese blocks together; press. Make 2 strips. <u>At this point each strip should measure 8-1/2 x 40-1/2"</u>.

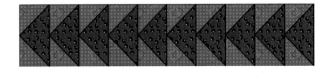

Make 2

Step 3 Sew the 2-1/2 x 40-1/2" **RED PRINT** strips to both long edges of each flying geese strip; press.

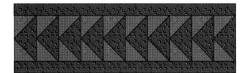

Make 2

Quilt Center

Cutting
From **RED FLORAL**:
- Cut 1, 20-1/2 x 40-1/2" rectangle
- Cut 2, 4-1/2 x 40-1/2" strips

Quilt Center Assembly

Step 1 Referring to the quilt diagram, sew the flying geese strips to both long edges of the 20-1/2 x 40-1/2" **RED FLORAL** rectangle; press.

Step 2 Sew the 4-1/2 x 40-1/2" **RED FLORAL** strips to the top and bottom of the Step 1 unit; press.

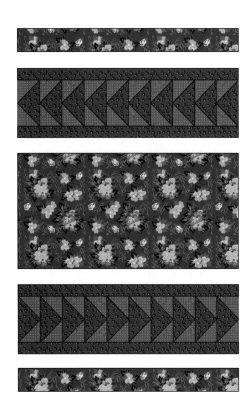

Borders

Note: The yardage given allows for the border strips to be cut on the crosswise grain. Diagonally piece the strips as needed, referring to Diagonal Piecing instructions on page 125. Read through Border instructions on page 125 for general instructions on adding borders.

Cutting
From **DARK GREEN PRINT**:
- Cut 6, 2-1/2 x 42" inner border strips

From **MEDIUM GREEN PRINT**:
- Cut 7, 10-1/2 x 42" outer border strips

Attaching the Borders

Step 1 Attach the 2-1/2" wide **DARK GREEN** inner border strips.

Step 2 Attach the 10-1/2" wide **MEDIUM GREEN** outer border strips.

Putting It All Together

Cut the 4-1/2 yard length of backing fabric in half crosswise to make 2, 2-1/4 yard lengths. Refer to Finishing the Quilt on page 126 for complete instructions.

Binding

Cutting
From **RED PRINT**:
- Cut 8, 6-1/2 x 42" strips

Sew the binding to the quilt using a scant 1" seam allowance. This measurement will produce a 1" wide finished double binding. Refer to Binding and Diagonal Piecing on page 127 for complete instructions.

Picnic Quilt

The Winter Quilt

Finished Size: 64 x 76"

Fabrics and Supplies

3 yards   **BEIGE/GREEN PLAID**
for center blocks and outer blocks

2 yards   **GREEN STRIPE**
for lattice and blocks

2/3 yard   **GREEN PLAID**
for lattice posts and corner squares

2 yards   **GREEN FLORAL** for blocks

2/3 yard   **BEIGE PRINT** for corner squares

1-7/8 yards   **GREEN FLORAL** for binding

7-1/8 yards   backing fabric

quilt batting, at least 84 x 98"

Quilt Center

Cutting

From **BEIGE/GREEN PLAID**:
- Cut 1, 12-1/2 x 42" strip. From the strip cut:
2, 12-1/2" squares

- Cut 10, 8-1/2 x 42" strips. From the strips cut:
2, 8-1/2 x 30-1/2" rectangles
10, 8-1/2 x 16-1/2" rectangles
6, 8-1/2 x 12-1/2" rectangles
4, 8-1/2" squares

From **GREEN STRIPE**:
- Cut 3, 8-1/2 x 42" strips. Diagonally piece
the strips and cut into:
2, 8-1/2 x 46-1/2" rectangles.

- Cut 3 more 8-1/2 x 42" strips.
From the strips cut:
2, 8-1/2 x 32-1/2" rectangles
4, 8-1/2" squares

- Cut 5, 2-1/2 x 42" strips. From the strips cut:
7, 2-1/2 x 12-1/2" rectangles
10, 2-1/2 x 8-1/2" rectangles

From **GREEN PLAID**:
- Cut 2, 8-1/2 x 42" strips. From the strips cut:
8, 8-1/2" squares
6, 2-1/2" squares

From **GREEN FLORAL**:
- Cut 3, 8-1/2 x 42" strips. Diagonally piece
the strips and cut into:
2, 8-1/2 x 46-1/2" rectangles.

- Cut 4 more 8-1/2 x 42" strips.
From the strips cut:
2, 8-1/2 x 32-1/2" rectangles
8, 8-1/2" squares

From **BEIGE PRINT**:
- Cut 2, 8-1/2 x 42" strips. From the strips cut:
8, 8-1/2" squares

Quilt Center Assembly

Step 1   Sew together the 12-1/2" **BEIGE/GREEN
PLAID** squares, 2 of the 8-1/2 x 12-1/2"
BEIGE/GREEN PLAID rectangles, and
3 of the 2-1/2 x 12-1/2" **GREEN STRIPE**
rectangles. Press the seam allowances
toward the **GREEN STRIPE** fabric.

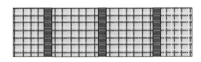

Make 1

Step 2   Sew together 3 of the 2-1/2"
GREEN PLAID squares, 2 of the
2-1/2 x 12-1/2" **GREEN STRIPE**
rectangles, and 2 of the 2-1/2 x 8-1/2"
GREEN STRIPE rectangles. Make 2
lattice strips. Press the seam allowances
toward the **GREEN STRIPE** fabric.
Sew the lattice strips to both side edges
of the Step 1 unit; press.

Make 2

Step 3   Sew together 2 of the 8-1/2 x 12-1/2"
BEIGE/GREEN PLAID rectangles,
2 of the 8-1/2" **BEIGE/GREEN PLAID**
squares, and 3 of the 2-1/2 x 8-1/2"

GREEN STRIPE rectangles. Press the seam allowances toward the **GREEN STRIPE** fabric. Make 2 units. Sew the units to both side edges of the quilt center; press. At this point the quilt center should measure 32-1/2 x 46-1/2".

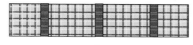

Make 2

Side Sections

Make 2

Step 1   Sew 8-1/2" **BEIGE PRINT** squares to both side edges of an 8-1/2 x 30-1/2" **BEIGE/GREEN PLAID** rectangle; press. Make 2 units.

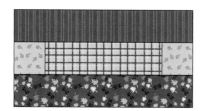

Make 2

Step 2   Sew an 8-1/2 x 46-1/2" **GREEN STRIPE** rectangle and a **GREEN FLORAL** rectangle to both side edges of a Step 1 unit; press. Make 2 units. Sew the units to both side edges of the quilt center; press.

Quilt Center Diagram

Top and Bottom Section

Make 2

Step 1   Sew 8-1/2" **BEIGE PRINT** squares to both side edges of an 8-1/2 x 16-1/2"

BEIGE/GREEN PLAID rectangle; press. Make 2 units.

Step 2   Sew an 8-1/2 x 32-1/2" **GREEN STRIPE** rectangle and a **GREEN FLORAL** rectangle to both side edges of a Step 1 unit; press. Make 2 units.

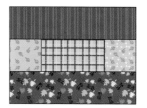

Make 2

Step 3   Sew together the 8-1/2" **GREEN FLORAL** and **GREEN PLAID** squares in pairs; press. Make 4 units. Sew together the 8-1/2" **GREEN FLORAL** and **GREEN STRIPE** squares in pairs; press. Make 4 units. Sew the units together to make 4 blocks; press. At this point each block should measure 16-1/2" square.

Make 4   *Make 4*

Make 4 blocks

Step 4   Sew an 8-1/2 x 16-1/2" **BEIGE/GREEN PLAID** rectangle to the top edge of each block; press. Sew an 8-1/2" **GREEN PLAID** square to each remaining **BEIGE/GREEN PLAID** rectangle; press. Sew the units together; press. At this point each block should measure 24-1/2" square.

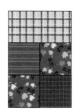 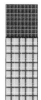 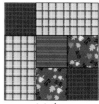

Make 4

Step 5 Sew the Step 4 units to both side edges of the Step 2 units; press. Sew the units to the top/bottom edges of the quilt center; press.

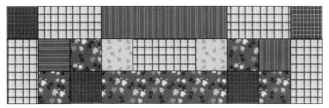

Make 1 for top and 1 for bottom

Putting It All Together

Cut the 7-1/8 yard length of backing fabric in thirds crosswise to make 3, 2-3/8 yard lengths.

Refer to Finishing the Quilt on page 126 for complete instructions.

Binding

Cutting

From **GREEN FLORAL**:
- Cut 9, 6-1/2 x 42" strips

Sew the binding to the quilt using a scant 1" seam allowance. This measurement will produce a 1" wide finished double binding. Refer to Binding and Diagonal Piecing on page 127 for complete instructions .

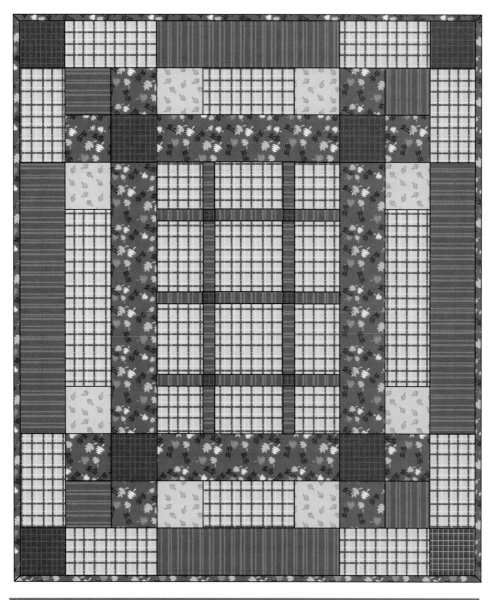

The Winter Quilt

Envelope Pillow

20" square

Fabrics and Supplies

(for one pillow covering)

20" square **GREEN PLAID** for pillow front

1-1/4 yards **GREEN PRINT** for pillow front and back

3/4 yard **ROSE PLAID** for binding (cut on the bias)

18" square pillow form

1" diameter button (optional covered button)

Pillow Top

Cutting

From **GREEN PLAID**:
- Cut 1, 18-1/2" square

From **GREEN PRINT**:
- Cut 2, 14-1/2 x 18-1/2" rectangles

From **ROSE PLAID** (diagonally piece the strips as needed):

- Cut enough 2-3/4" wide bias strips to make a 25" long binding strip.

- Cut enough 2-3/4" wide bias strips to make an 85" long binding strip.

Set this strip aside to be used for binding the outer edge of the pillow.

Piecing

Step 1 With wrong sides together, layer the 14-1/2 x 18-1/2" **GREEN PRINT** rectangles. Refer to the diagram below to cut the angle. Baste the 2 layers together a scant 1/4" from the edge to create a single angled piece.

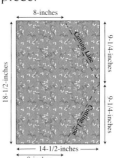

Step 2 To bind the angled edge with the 2-3/4 x 25" bias **ROSE PLAID** strip, refer to the diagram below and page 127 for Binding and Diagonal Piecing Instructions.

Step 3 Layer the bound **GREEN PRINT** angled unit on the 18-1/2" **GREEN PRINT** square; with right sides facing up so that the pillow top measures 18-1/2" square; and pin. Baste the layers together a scant 1/4" from the edge to create the pillow top. Sew the button to the pillow top, stitching through all the layers.

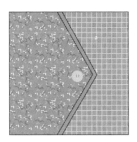

Pillow Back

Cutting

From **GREEN PRINT**:
• Cut 2, 18-1/2 x 22" rectangles

Assembling the Pillow Back

Step 1 With wrong sides together, fold each 18-1/2 x 22" **GREEN PRINT** rectangle in half to make 2, 11 x 18-1/2" double-thick pillow back pieces.

Step 2 Overlap the 2 folded edges so the pillow back measures 18-1/2" square; pin. Stitch around the entire square to create a single pillow back, using a 1/4" seam allowance.

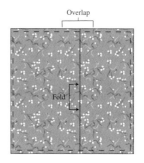

Step 3 With wrong sides together, layer the pillow back and the pillow top; pin. Stitch around the entire pillow using a 3/8" seam allowance.

Note: The finishing technique used on this pillow is the same as binding a small quilt with double-fold binding, mitering the corners. This is much easier than inserting a thick, covered cording at the pillow edge.

Binding

Sew the 2-3/4 x 85" bias **ROSE PLAID** binding to the pillow using a 3/8" seam allowance. This measurement will produce a 1/2" wide finished double binding. Refer to page 127 for Binding and Diagonal Piecing Instructions.

Insert the pillow form through the back opening.

General Instructions

- Yardage is based on 42-inch wide fabric. If your fabric is wider or narrower it will affect the amount of necessary strips you need to cut in some patterns, and of course, it will affect the amount of fabric you have left over. Generally, THIMBLEBERRIES® patterns allow for a little extra fabric so you can confidently cut your pattern pieces with ease.

- A rotary cutter, mat, and wide clear plastic ruler with 1/8-inch markings are needed tools in attaining accuracy. A beginner needs good tools just as an experienced quilt maker needs good equipment. A 24 x 36-inch mat board is a good size to own. It will easily accommodate the average quilt fabrics and will aid in accurate cutting. The plastic ruler you purchase should be at least 6 x 24-inches and easy to read. Do not purchase a smaller ruler to save money, the large size will be invaluable to your quilt making success.

- It is often recommended to prewash and press fabrics to test for color fastness and possible shrinkage. If you choose to prewash, wash in cool water and dry in a cool to moderate dryer. Industry standards actually suggest that line drying is best. Shrinkage is generally very minimal and usually is not a concern. A good way to test your fabric for both shrinkage and color fastness is to cut a 3-inch square of fabric. Soak the fabric in a white bowl filled with water. Squeeze the water out of the fabric and press it dry on a piece of muslin. If the fabric is going to release color it will do so either in the water or when it is pressed dry. Re-measure the 3-inch fabric square to see if it has changed size considerably (more than 1/4-inch). If it has, wash, dry, and press the entire yardage. This little test could save you hours in prewashing and pressing.

- Read instructions thoroughly before beginning a project. Each step will make more sense to you when you have a general overview of the whole process. Take one step at time and follow the illustrations. They will often make more sense to you than the words. Take "baby steps" so you don't get overwhelmed by the entire process.

- When working with flannel and other loosely woven fabrics, always prewash and dry. These fabrics almost always shrink some.

- For piecing, place right sides of the fabric pieces together and use 1/4-inch seam allowances throughout the entire quilt unless otherwise specifically stated in the directions. An accurate seam allowance is the most important part of the quilt making process after accurate cutting. All the directions are based on accurate 1/4-inch seam allowances. It is very important to check your sewing machine to see what position your fabric should be to get accurate seams. To test, use a piece of 1/4-inch graph paper, stitch along the quarter inch line as if the paper where fabric. Make note of where the edge of the paper lines up with your presser foot or where it lines up on the throat plate of your machine. Many quilters place a piece of masking tape on the throat plate to help guide the edge of the fabric. Now test your seam allowance on fabric. Cut 2, 2-1/2-inch squares, place right sides together and stitch along one edge. Press seam allowances in one direction and measure. <u>At this point the unit should measure 2-1/2 x 4-1/2-inches</u>. If it does not, adjust your stitching guidelines and test again. Seam allowances are included in the cutting sizes given in this book.

• Pressing is the third most important step in quilt making. As a general rule, you should never cross a stitched seam with another seam unless it has been pressed. Therefore, every time you stitch a seam it needs to be pressed before adding another piece. Often, it will feel like you press as much as you sew, and often that is true. It is very important that you press and not iron the seams. Pressing is a firm, up and down motion that will flatten the seams but not distort the piecing. Ironing is a back and forth motion and will stretch and distort the small pieces. Most quilters use steam to help the pressing process. The moisture does help and will not distort the shapes as long as the pressing motion is used.

• An old fashioned rule is to press seam allowances in one direction, toward the darker fabric. Often, background fabrics are light in color and pressing toward the darker fabric prevents the seam allowances from showing through to the right side. Pressing seam allowances in one direction is thought to create a stronger seam. Also, for ease in hand-quilting, the quilting lines should fall on the side of the seam which is opposite the seam allowance. As you piece quilts, you will find these "rules" to be helpful but not necessarily always appropriate. Sometimes seams need to be pressed in the opposite direction so the seams of different units will fit together more easily which quilters refer to as seams "nesting" together. When sewing together two units with opposing seam allowances, use the tip of your seam ripper to gently guide the units under your presser foot. Sometimes it is necessary to re-press the seams to make the units fit together nicely. Always try to achieve the least bulk in one spot and accept that no matter which way you press, it may be a little tricky and it could be a little bulky.

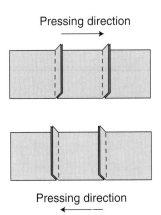

Pressing direction

Pressing direction

Squaring Up Blocks

To square up your blocks, first check the seam allowances. This is usually where the problem is, and it is always best to alter within the block rather than trim the outer edges. Next, make sure you have pressed accurately. Sometimes a block can become distorted by ironing instead of pressing.

To trim up block edges, use one of many clear plastic squares available on the market. Determine the center of the block; mark with a pin. Lay the square over the block and align as many perpendicular and horizontal lines as you can to the seams in your block. This will indicate where the block is off. Do not trim all off on one side; this usually results in real distortion of the pieces in the block and the block design. Take a little off all sides until the block is square. When assembling many blocks, it it necessary to make sure all are the same size.

Tools and Equipment

Making beautiful quilts does not require a large number of specialized tools or expensive equipment. My list of favorites is short and sweet, and includes the things I use over and over again because they are always accurate and dependable.

- I find a long acrylic ruler indispensable for accurate rotary cutting. The ones I like most are an Omnigrid 6 x 24-inch grid acrylic ruler for cutting long strips and squaring up fabrics and quilt tops, and a Master Piece® 45, 8 x 24-inch ruler for cutting 6- to 8-inch wide borders. I sometimes tape together two 6 x 24-inch acrylic rulers for cutting borders up to 12-inches wide.

- A 15-inch Omnigrid® square acrylic ruler is great for squaring up individual blocks and corners of a quilt top, for cutting strips up to 15-inches wide or long, and for trimming side and corner triangles.

- I think the markings on my 24 x 36-inch Olfa rotary cutting mat stay visible longer than on other mats, and the lines are fine and accurate.

- The largest size Olfa rotary cutter cuts through many layers of fabric easily, and it isn't cumbersome to use. The 2-1/2-inch blade slices through three layers of backing, batting, and a quilt top like butter.

- An 8-inch pair of Gingher shears is great for cutting out applique templates and cutting fabric from a bolt or fabric scraps.

- I keep a pair of 5-1/4-inch Gingher scissors by my sewing machine, so it is handy for both machine work and handwork. This size is versatile and sharp enough to make large and small cuts equally well.

- My Grabbit® magnetic pin cushion has a surface that is large enough to hold lots of straight pins, and a strong magnet that keeps them securely in place.

- Silk pins are long and thin, which means they won't leave large holes in your fabric. I like them because they increase accuracy in pinning pieces or blocks together, and it is easy to press over silk pins, as well.

- For pressing individual pieces, blocks, and quilt tops, I use an 18 x 48-inch sheet of plywood covered with several layers of cotton fiberfill and topped with a layer of muslin stapled to the back. The 48-inch length allows me to press an entire width of fabric at one time without the need to reposition it, and the square ends are better than tapered ends on an ironing board for pressing finished quilt tops.

Rotary Cutting

- Safety First! The blades of a rotary cutter are very sharp and need to be for accurate cutting. Look at a variety of cutters to find one that feels good in your hand. All quality cutters have a safety mechanism to "close" the cutting blade when not in use. After each cut and before laying the rotary cutter down, close the blade. Soon this will become second nature to you and will prevent dangerous accidents. Always keep cutters out of the sight of children. Rotary cutters are very tempting to fiddle with when they are laying around. When your blade is dull or nicked, change it. Damaged blades do not cut accurately and require extra effort that can also result in slipping and injury. Also, always cut away from yourself for safety.

- Fold the fabric in half lengthwise matching the selvage edges.

- "Square off" the ends of your fabric before measuring and cutting pieces. This means that the cut edge of the fabric must be exactly perpendicular to the folded edge which creates a 90° angle. Align the folded and selvage edges of the fabric with the lines on the cutting board, and place a ruled square on the fold. Place a 6 x 24-inch ruler against the side of the square to get a 90° angle. Hold the ruler in place, remove the square, and cut along the edge of the ruler. If you are left-handed, work from the

other end of the fabric. Use the lines on your cutting board to help line up fabric, but not to measure and cut strips. Use a ruler for accurate cutting, always checking to make sure your fabric is lined up with horizontal and vertical lines on the ruler.

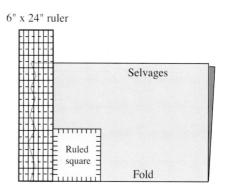

6" x 24" ruler

Selvages

Ruled square

Fold

Cutting Strips

- When cutting strips or rectangles, cut on the crosswise grain. Strips can then be cut into squares or smaller rectangles.

- If your strips are not straight after cutting a few of them, refold the fabric, align the folded and selvage edges with the lines on the cutting board, and "square off" the edge again by trimming to straighten, and begin cutting.

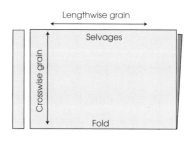

Lengthwise grain

Selvages

Crosswise grain

Fold

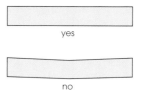

yes

no

Cutting Side and Corner Triangles

In projects with side and corner triangles, the instructions have you cut side and corner triangles larger than needed. This will allow you to square up the quilt and eliminates the frustration of ending up with precut side and corner triangles that don't match the size of your pieced blocks.

To cut triangles, first cut squares. The project directions will tell you what size to make the squares and whether to cut them in half to make two triangles or to cut them in quarters to make four triangles, as shown in the diagrams. This cutting method will give you side triangles that have the straight of grain on the outside edges of the quilt. This is a very important part of quilt making that will help stabilize your quilt center.

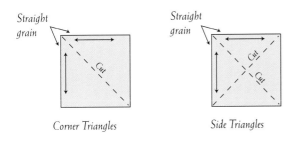

Corner Triangles   Side Triangles

Begin at a corner by lining up your ruler 1/4-inch beyond the points of the corners of the blocks as shown. Cut along the edge of the ruler. Repeat this procedure on all four sides of the quilt top.

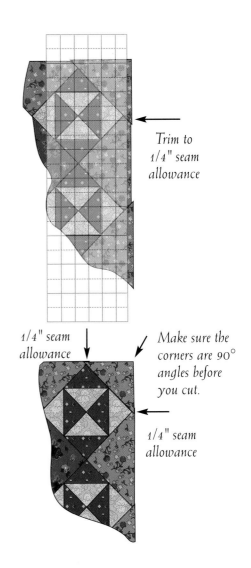

Trim to 1/4" seam allowance

1/4" seam allowance

Make sure the corners are 90° angles before you cut.

1/4" seam allowance

Sewing with Flannel

- Always prewash and machine dry flannel. This will prevent severe shrinkage after the quilt is made. Some flannels shrink more than others. For this reason, we have allowed approximately 1/4 yard extra for each fabric under the fabric requirements. Treat the more heavily napped side of solid flannels as the right side of the fabric.

- Because flannel stretches more than other cotton calicos and because the nap makes them thicker, the quilt design should be simple. Let the fabric and color make the design statement.

- Consider combining regular cotton calicos with flannels. The different textures complement each other nicely.

- Use a 10 to 12 stitches per inch setting on your machine. A 1/4-inch seam allowance is also recommended for flannel piecing.

- When sewing triangle-pieced squares together, take extra care not to stretch the diagonal seam. Trim off the points from the seam allowances to eliminate bulk.

- Press gently to prevent stretching pieces out of shape.

- Check block measurements as you progress. "Square up" the blocks as needed. Flannel will shift and it is easy to end up with blocks that are misshapen. If you trim and measure as you go, you are more likely to have accurate blocks.

- If you notice a piece of flannel is stretching more than the others, place it on the bottom when stitching on the machine. The natural action of the feed dogs will help prevent it from stretching.

- Before stitching pieces, strips, or borders together, pin often to prevent fabric from stretching and moving. When stitching longer pieces together, divide the pieces into quarters and pin. Divide into even smaller sections to get more control.

- Use a lightweight batting to prevent the quilt from becoming too heavy.

Cutting accurate triangles can be intimidating, but a clear plastic ruler, rotary cutter, and cutting mat are all that are needed to make perfect triangles. The cutting instructions often direct you to cut strips, then squares, and then triangles

Sewing Layered Strips Together

When you are instructed to layer strips, right sides together, and sew, you need to take some precautions. Gently lay a strip on top of another carefully lining up the raw edges. Pressing the strips together will hold them together nicely and a few pins here and there will also help. Be careful not to stretch the strips as you sew them together.

Hints & Helps for Pressing Strip Sets

When sewing strips of fabric together for strip sets, it is important to press the seam allowances nice and flat, usually to the dark fabric. Be careful not to stretch as you press, causing a "rainbow effect." This will affect the accuracy and shape of the pieces cut from the strip set. I like to press on the wrong side first and with the strips perpendicular to the ironing board. Then I flip the piece over and press on the right side to prevent little pleats from forming at the seams. Laying the strip set lengthwise on the ironing board seems to encourage the rainbow effect, as shown in diagram.

Avoid this rainbow effect

Rod Casing or Sleeve to Hang Quilts

To hang wall quilts, attach a casing that is made of the same fabric as the quilt back. Attach this casing at the top of the quilt, just below the binding. Often, it is helpful to attach a second casing at the bottom of the quilt so you can insert a dowel into it which will help weight the quilt and make it hang free of ripples.

To make a rod casing or "sleeve", cut enough strips of fabric equal to the width of the quilt plus 2-inches for side hems. Generally, 6-inch wide strips will accommodate most rods. If you are using a rod with a larger diameter, increase the width of the strips.

Seam the strips together to get the length needed; press. Fold the strip in half lengthwise, wrong sides together. Stitch the long raw edges together with a 1/4-inch seam allowance. Center the seam on the backside of the sleeve; press. The raw edges of the seam will be concealed when the sleeve is stitched to the back of the quilt. Turn under both of the short raw edges; press and stitch to hem the ends. The final measurement should be about 1/2-inch from the quilt edges.

Pin the sleeve to the back of the quilt so the top edge of the sleeve is just below the binding. Hand-stitch the top edge of the sleeve in place, then the bottom edge. Make sure to knot and secure your stitches at each end of the sleeve to make sure it will not pull away from the quilt with use. Slip the rod into the casing. If your wall quilt is not directional, making a sleeve for the bottom edge will allow you to turn your quilt end to end to relieve the stress at the top edge. You could also slip a dowel into the bottom sleeve to help anchor the lower edge of the wall quilt.

Hand-stitch the sleeve to the quilt back

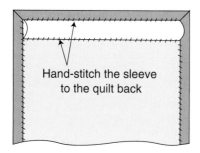

Choosing a Quilt Design

Quilting is such an individual process that it is difficult to recommend designs for each quilt. There are hundreds of quilting stencils available at quilt shops. (Templates are used generally for applique shapes; stencils are used for marking quilting designs.)

There are a few suggestion that may help you decide how to quilt your project, depending on how much time you would like to spend quilting. Many quilters now use professional long arm quilting machines or hire someone skilled at running these machines to do the quilting. This, of course, frees up more time to piece.

Quilting Suggestions

- Repeat one of the design elements in the quilt as part of the quilting design.

- Two or three parallel rows of echo quilting outside an applique piece will highlight the shape.

- Stipple or meander quilting behind a feather or central motif will make the primary design more prominent.

- Look for quilting designs that will cover two or more borders, rather than choosing separate designs for each individual border.

- Quilting in the ditch of seams is an effective way to get a project quilted without a great deal of time marking the quilt.

Marking the Quilting Design

When marking the quilt top, use a marking tool that will be visible on the quilt fabric and yet will be easy enough to remove. Always test your marking tool on a scrap of fabric before marking the entire quilt.

Along with a multitude of commercial marking tools available, you may find that very thin slivers of hand soap (Dial, Ivory, etc.) work really well for marking medium to dark color fabrics. The thin lines of soap show up nicely and they are easily removed by simply rubbing gently with a piece of like colored fabric.

Quilt Backing Basics

Yardage Requirements and Piecing Suggestions

Crib 45 x 60"

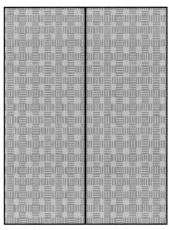

2-3/4 yards
Cut 2, 1-3/8 yard
lengths

Twin 72" x 90"

5-1/4 yards
Cut 2, 2-5/8 yard lengths

Double/Full 81 x 96"

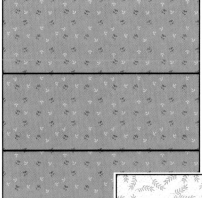

7-1/8 yards
Cut 3, 2-3/8 yard
lengths

Queen 90 x 108"

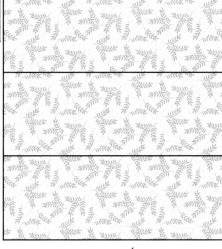

8 yards
Cut 3, 2-5/8 yard lengths

Borders

Note . . .

The diagonal seams disguise the piecing better than straight seams. The exception is when a woven plaid is used for a border. It is then best to cut the border strips on the lengthwise grain (parallel to the selvages). When sewing on the bias, sew slowly and do not use too small of a stitch which could cause stretching of the fabric.

Diagonal Piecing

Stitch diagonally   *Trim to 1/4" seam allowance*   *Press seam open*

Step 1 With pins, mark the center points along all 4 sides of the quilt. For the top and bottom borders measure the quilt from left to right through the middle. This measurement will give you the most accurate measurement that will result in a "square" quilt.

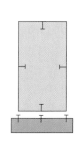

Step 2 Measure and mark the border lengths and center points on the strips cut for the borders before sewing them on.

Step 3 Pin the border strips to the quilt matching the pinned points on each of the borders and the quilt. Pin borders every 6 to 8-inches easing the fabric to fit as necessary. This will prevent the borders and quilt center from stretching while you are sewing them together. Stitch a 1/4-inch seam. Press the seam allowance toward the borders. Trim off excess border lengths.

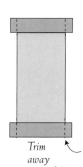

Trim away excess fabric

Step 4 For the side borders, measure your quilt from top to bottom, including the borders just added, to determine the length of the side borders.

Step 5 Measure and mark the side border lengths as you did for the top and bottom borders.

Step 6 Pin and stitch the side border strips in place. When attaching the last two side outer border strips, taking a few backstitches at the beginning and the end of the border will help keep the quilt borders intact during the quilting process. Press and trim the border strips even with the borders just added.

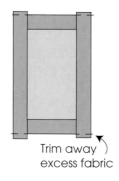

Trim away
excess fabric

Step 7 If your quilt has multiple borders, measure, mark, and sew additional borders to the quilt in the same manner.

Finishing the Quilt

Now that your quilt is finished it needs to be layered with batting and backing, and prepared for quilting. Whether it is machine-quilted or hand-quilted, it is best to baste all 3 layers together. You may hand-baste with large basting stitches or pin-baste with medium size brass safety pins. Many quilters are satisfied with spray adhesives which are available at local quilt shops.

Step 1 Press the completed quilt top on the backside first, carefully clipping and removing hanging threads. Then press the quilt front making sure all seams are flat and all loose threads are removed.

Step 2 Remove the selvages from the backing fabric. Sew the long edges together; press. Trim the backing and batting so they are 4-inches larger than the quilt top.

Step 3 Mark the quilt top for quilting. Layer the backing, batting, and quilt top. Baste the 3 layers together and quilt. Work from the center of the quilt out to the edges. This will help keep the quilt flat by working the excess of the 3 layers to the outside edges.

Step 4 When quilting is complete, remove basting. Hand-baste the 3 layers together a scant 1/4-inch from the edge. This basting keeps the layers from shifting and prevents puckers from forming when adding the binding. Trim excess batting and backing fabric even with the edge of the quilt top.

Borders with Corner Squares

Step 1 For the top and bottom borders, refer to Steps 1, 2, and 3 in Border Instructions on page 125. Measure, mark, and sew the top and bottom borders to the quilt. Trim away the excess fabric.

Step 2 For the side borders, measure just the quilt top including seam allowances, but not the top and bottom borders. Cut the side borders to this length. Sew a corner square to each end of these border strips. Sew the borders to the quilt, and press.